CALKE ABBEY

THE NATIONAL TRUST

This book has been the work of many contributors, to whom the National Trust is very grateful. Howard Colvin, former Reader in Architectural History at Oxford University, wrote the first three chapters. The chapter on the contents of Calke was compiled from the research of Catherine Wills on the paintings (aided by Howard Colvin, Sir Oliver Millar and Alastair Laing); David Clements, formerly of the Trust's biological survey, and Michael Seago on the natural history collections; and Christopher Nicholson, the Trust's adviser on conservation of carriages, on the carriages. The chapter on the rescue of Calke was written by John Chesshyre, formerly the Trust's Historic Buildings Representative for the East Midlands. The Tour of the House was compiled from notes by John Chesshyre, Catherine Wills and Philip Heath, who has made a special study of the Calke archives. The chapters on the park, gardens and estate were written by Philip Heath. Many other members of the National Trust staff have also given their valuable expert advice.

Margaret Willes, *The Publisher*

Photographs: Howard Colvin pages 74, 83; Mellon Foundation 25; Derry Moore 44; Royal Commission on the Historical Monuments of England 11, 20; National Trust 17 right & left, 18, 19, 26, 34, 51, 75 above, 89; NT/Christopher Dalton 32 above, 38, 39 below, 42, 54, 80; NT/Mark Fiennes 70, 71 above; NT/Mike Freeman 27, 33 right & left, 37, 64; NT/Angelo Hornak 13 left & right, 15; NT/Chris Hurst 30 left, 31, 49, 50 right & left above, 65; NT/Lucinda Lambton 71 below, 72, 82 above; NT/Dennis Mansell 43; NT/Mr Middleton 41 right; NT/Kerry Usher 9, 24 right, 41 left, 76, 82 below, 88; NT/Roger Walkinton 50 below; NT/ Mike Williams front & back covers, 4, 7, 12, 14 below & above, 16, 21, 24 left, 29, 30 right, 32 below, 35 below & above, 36, 39 above, 46, 57, 61, 67, 68, 75 below, 77, 78, 79, 81, 84, 85, 87; Sotheby's 8; World of Interiors/ Richard Davies 6; George Wright 40; Yale Center for British Art, New Haven 25

First published in Great Britain in 1989 by the National Trust

Copyright © 1989 The National Trust
Registered charity no. 205846
Reprinted with corrections 1990, 1991, 1993, 1996

ISBN 0 7078 0099 4

Designed by James Shurmer

Phototypeset in Monotype Bembo Series 270
by Southern Positives and Negatives (SPAN), Lingfield Surrey (10036)

Colour reproductions by Acculith 76, Barnet, Hertfordshire

Printed in Italy by Amilcare Pizzi s.p.a. for
National Trust Enterprises Limited, 36 Queen Anne's Gate,
London SW1H 9AS

CONTENTS

INTRODUCTION

When the National Trust took over Calke Abbey in 1985, the event attracted great national interest. Articles headed 'The house where time stood still' or 'A time capsule' appeared in the press, and a book was published with the subtitle 'A Hidden House Revealed'. A year earlier, on 13 March 1984, the Chancellor of the Exchequer had announced in his budget statement in the House of Commons that the National Heritage Memorial Fund was to be given an extra sum of money so that Calke Abbey could pass to the Trust; it was an unprecedented reference. And the public rose magnificently to the occasion, responding to the Trust's appeal for $£\frac{1}{4}$ million, and even doubling it.

Yet Calke Abbey, although a fine Baroque house, is not of top-ranking architectural importance like nearby Kedleston, which two years later also passed to the care of the Trust. Parallels were drawn with Erddig, the house near Wrexham rescued by the Trust in the 1970s, but Calke's furniture and furnishings could not compare. The park is lovely, but no comparison with Studley Royal in Yorkshire, another recent Trust acquisition. So why all the fuss?

The unique quality of Calke lies with the family that has lived there since the reign of James I, the Harpur Crewes. The family's origins were conventional: wealth based on law was built up by clever marriages to enable Sir John Harpur in the opening years of the eighteenth century to build a fine house in a large park and to move in county circles. But less than a century later, his descendant Sir Henry, who changed his name to Crewe in 1808, was showing marked signs of oddness. Although keen to secure himself a peerage, he upset social conventions by marrying a lady's maid and, by cutting himself off from society, became known in his lifetime as the 'isolated baronet'.

His reclusive nature re-emerged in strong form in his great-grandson, Sir Vauncey Harpur Crewe, who was descended from him through both parents. In Sir Vauncey could be found all the most marked characteristics of the family: reclusiveness, a passion for collecting and an absorbing fascination with natural history. His tenure of Calke stamped these characteristics indelibly upon the house and estate.

When his grandson, Mr Henry Harpur-Crewe, handed over the house to the National Trust, Calke was virtually as Sir Vauncey had left it at his death in 1924,

Calke Abbey, south front

and in many ways as it had been when he inherited in 1886. Life in a late Victorian household was revealed to the public gaze; time had stood still.

As room after room yielded up the possessions of the Harpur Crewes, so their instinct for accumulation came to light: paintings, natural history specimens, stuffed animals, 'antiquities', carriages, and individual treasures like the magnificent State Bed. Here was a family who threw nothing away, but simply stored their treasures in a room and shut the door.

This book sets out to convey to the reader and the visitor some of the characteristics that make Calke Abbey unique. After an intensive programme of repair, the house, its contents and the park and gardens are now secure, and open for the first time to the general public. Calke Abbey is indeed a hidden house revealed.

The Drawing Room at Calke Abbey

CHAPTER ONE
CALKE PRIORY

Like many other English country houses, Calke Abbey stands on the site, and incorporates some of the fabric, of a medieval religious house that was secularised in the reign of Henry VIII. Calke Priory (it was never an 'Abbey', a name given to the present house only in 1808) was a house of Augustinian canons regular – that is, of men bound by religious vows to follow a rule (*regula*) attributed to St Augustine of Hippo, the celebrated fifth-century North African bishop. Although similar in many respects to Benedictine monks, Augustinian canons were not so strictly confined to their cloisters and undertook a certain amount of pastoral work. Each Augustinian house was ruled by an abbot or prior, and formed an independent religious community with its own landed endowment. There were about 200 Augustinian houses in England and Wales, of which the best known included Christ-church Priory in Hampshire, Dunstable Priory in Bedfordshire, Waltham Abbey in Essex, St Frideswide's Priory (now the Cathedral) in Oxford, and St Bartholomew's Priory in Smithfield, London. In Derbyshire there were Augustinian monasteries at Breadsall, Darley and Church Gresley, and there was another almost within sight of Calke at Breedon-on-the-Hill in Leicestershire.

Most of these Augustinian monasteries were founded in the twelfth century, at a time when a combination of social and religious pressures led many men and women to leave the world for a life of prayer and devotion. Some of them were drop-outs from a secular society whose values they rejected, while others were clergy who were persuaded by religious reformers to follow a monastic regime in accordance with the stricter standards then current in the Church. All of them had in principle renounced the secular world and vowed to live a communal life based on personal poverty, sexual abstinence and obedience to their abbot or prior.

Although each religious order set its own standards and had its own *esprit-de-corps*, it had to appeal to secular patronage for the landed endowment which sustained its individual houses. The patronage of the great tended to focus on one particular order which for a generation would enjoy their bounty before losing its appeal in the face of some newer and stricter manifestation of religious zeal. In England the order favoured by the first generation of Norman barons after the Conquest was the Benedictines, but by the middle of the twelfth century they had given way in aristocratic esteem to the Cistercians. The Augustinian canons were especially favoured by King Henry I (1100–35) and his courtiers, and it was to an Anglo-Norman baron closely associated with Henry that Calke Priory owed its foundation. He was Richard, 2nd Earl of Chester, a young man who in 1101 had inherited vast estates in England and Normandy from his father Earl Hugh D'Avranches. The heart of his English lands was in Cheshire, but many

A twelfth-century corbel from the Augustinian priory at Calke

Writ from Henry I to the Earl of Chester confirming to the canons of Calke the title of their land and other properties. Written in Latin in the 1130s

manors on the borders of Derbyshire and Leicestershire also belonged to him, including Calke, Repton, Ticknall, Smisby and Newton Solney. At the time of his father's death he was only seven years old. He came of age in 1115, and in 1120 he was one of the victims of the loss of the White Ship when a well-equipped shipload of courtiers was lost through the negligence of its crew; amongst those who drowned was the King's son and heir. Some time during the previous five years Richard had decided to found at Calke an Augustinian priory dedicated to St Giles. No foundation charter has been preserved, but later earls of Chester confirmed their predecessor's grants to the canons of Calke, and Henry I and his grandson, Henry II, both gave the priory royal protection. A letter of Henry II to this effect is one of the earliest documents to be preserved in the Harpur-Crewe archives.

As an independent religious community Calke Priory lasted for no more than half a century. After the death of the 5th Earl of Chester in 1153, some or all of the Derbyshire estate that he had inherited formed part of the dowry of his widow Matilda. Early in the reign of Henry II (1154–89) the Countess Matilda made arrangements for the canons of Calke to move to Repton, five miles away to the north west. It may be that Calke had proved to be in some way unsatisfactory as the site of a priory, but the fact that before the Danish invasions of the ninth century there had been a celebrated Anglo-Saxon monastery at Repton no doubt influenced her decision. In this way the Countess became in effect the founder of the new priory of Repton and by 1172 Calke had ceased to exist as an independent religious house. It continued, however, to serve as a 'cell' to Repton, that is as a subordinate establishment with less than a full complement of canons in residence. How long it maintained that status is not clear; by the later Middle Ages it is possible that Calke was more important as the centre of an agricultural estate than as a religious community, but of its history in the fourteenth and fifteenth centuries little is known.

In the reign of Henry I, however, we must envisage Calke Priory as the home of a dozen or more canons, distinguished from the members of other religious orders by their black outer garment. The buildings they occupied would have conformed to a standard layout of which the principal components were a church, a chapter-house, a refectory and a dormitory, grouped round a cloister. All these buildings must have been envisaged when the priory was founded, and it is likely that some if not all of them were completed before the move to Repton. How far they remained in use until the dissolution of the parent monastery in 1538 is another matter. By the early sixteenth century the former priory may well have looked more like a manor-house than a monastery. Whatever its form or appearance in the last days of English monasticism, there is every reason to suppose that Calke Priory occupied the site of the present mansion and that some of its foundations remain embedded in the latter's fabric.

When Repton Priory was dissolved in 1538 all its property was confiscated by the Crown. However, in anticipation of that event, the canons had granted long leases of some of their estates for a nominal rent in return for cash down. So on 29 August 1537 they leased their 'manor or cell' of Calke to one John Prest or Priest for 99 years, the rent for the first 59 years being prepaid. Prest was a member of the London Grocers' Company who evidently wished to retire to the country. He lived at Calke until his death in 1546, whereupon he was suceeded first by his widow and then by his daughter Frances and her husband William Bradbourne.

Meanwhile, the reversion of the lease had been granted by the Crown to John Dudley, Earl of Warwick. After passing through several hands, both freehold and leasehold interests in Calke were eventually acquired by Richard Wendsley or Wennesley. Wendsley was a member of an old Derbyshire family which took its name from Wensley in Darley Dale. He was an enterprising man who

had twice been MP for Derbyshire and he was actively engaged in the marketing of lead from mines in the Peak District. Having bought Calke, he 'did build divers edifices thereupon and did inhabit and dwell upon the same'. However, in 1585 he sold the estate to a lawyer, Robert Bainbridge, who was MP for Derby in 1571, 1572 and 1586. He was one of the extreme Protestant Members who refused to accept the Elizabethan Church Settlement and in 1586 he so infuriated Queen Elizabeth by his uncompromising attitude that he was sent to the Tower of London, where his initials can still be seen cut on the wall of the Beauchamp Tower in which he was confined. It is possible that Calke appealed to him as a residence because, like some other parishes that had formerly been in the hands of religious orders, it was a 'peculiar' exempt from the jurisdiction of the bishop and therefore a place where he could worship in the Puritan manner without any interference. After his death in 1613 Calke went to his son Robert, who in 1622 sold the estate to Henry Harpur for £5,350.

One of the monastic occupants of Calke Priory: a medieval adult male skeleton uncovered by archaeologists in the course of excavation for drains and electricity cables

CHAPTER TWO

THE HARPUR FAMILY

Although Calke became Harpur property in 1622, the family had been established in Derbyshire since the middle of the previous century. Its founder was Richard Harpur, a successful lawyer who rose to be one of the judges of the Court of Common Pleas at Westminster and was in addition Chief Justice of the County Palatine of Lancaster. In the course of his career he built up a considerable landed estate in many parts of England, but principally in Derbyshire and Staffordshire. The Staffordshire estate, centred on Alstonefield, north of Ashbourne, was acquired by purchase, but most of the Derbyshire estate Richard Harpur gained by marriage to the heiress of the Finderns, a family who had lived for centuries at the village 5 miles south-west of Derby from which they took their name. Richard Harpur probably married Jane Findern in the late 1540s, and in 1558 the death without children of her brother Thomas made Richard and Jane the owners of lands in Findern, Swarkestone, Repton, Ticknall, Twyford, Stanton-by-Bridge and elsewhere in south Derbyshire. It was at Swarkestone rather than at Findern that Richard Harpur chose to build a new house for himself, and when he died in January 1577 he was buried in Swarkestone Church in a chapel he had built. There the alabaster tomb of Richard Harpur and his wife can still be seen. It is a late and clumsy product of a firm of carvers at Burton-upon-Trent called Roiley, but Richard's effigy is correctly clothed in the robes of an Elizabethan judge and his head is encased in the close-fitting cap or coif that was the distinguishing headgear of a serjeant-at-law, a legal status that he had attained in 1558. Round his neck is the collar or chain that he would have worn as Chief Justice.

Richard and Jane Harpur left two sons, John and Richard. John, the elder, inherited Swarkestone and the bulk of his father's estate, while Richard was set up as lord of the manor of Littleover near Derby. There his descendants continued to live until that branch of the family became extinct in the middle of the eighteenth century.

Although he had legal training, John Harpur had no need to earn his living by the practice of the law. He devoted himself to the management of his property and to the pursuits of a country gentleman. By 1573 he was a Justice of the Peace and he soon became deeply involved in local affairs, both as an agent of central government and as the right-hand man of the earls of Shewsbury, who were then the leading magnates in Derbyshire. It was not always easy to serve both with equal loyalty and diligence; in 1595 John Harpur got into serious trouble by failing to act with sufficient vigour against another of the Earl of Shewsbury's followers who had been denounced as a 'Papist and recusant' by Robert Bainbridge, the ultra-Protestant owner of Calke. As a result Harpur was summoned to London and sent to the Fleet Prison, whence he addressed a series of abject letters to Sir Robert Cecil, the Secretary of State, protesting his loyalty to the Queen, his adhesion to the Protestant faith, and his penitence for his 'late error and great oversight'. His disgrace was only temporary, for in 1597 he was elected as one of the MPs for Derbyshire and in 1603 he was knighted by James I. By the time of his death in 1622 he was one of the best known and most respected figures in the county. The poet Thomas Bancroft composed an epigram in his memory, and he and his wife, Isabella Pierrepont, lie in the Harpur Chapel at Swarkestone beneath effigies of local alabaster carved by an unknown sculptor of some ability.

Sir John Harpur had five daughters and seven sons, four of whom died young. Each of the three survivors was provided with his own estate: Richard at Hemington in Leicestershire; John at

Breadsall, near Derby, the heiress to which he married; and Henry at Calke. However, a series of deaths in 1619–22 deprived the family of the eldest son, Richard, of the younger, John, of Richard's heir, another John, and finally of old Sir John himself. As a result John Harpur's son, John, inherited not only his father's estate at Breadsall, but Swarkestone and all his grandfather's lands in Derbyshire and Staffordshire as well.

The new head of the Harpur family had barely come of age before the tensions that were to lead to the Civil War began to build up around him. As a Royalist he found himself in a difficult position in a county where the King's exactions were strongly resisted. In 1636 he was appointed Sheriff and in that capacity had responsibility for collecting the hated 'Ship Money'. In 1643 the Parliamentary leader Sir John Gell captured Swarkestone Bridge and the Harpur mansion may have suffered some slight damage. More serious were the fines totalling £4,583 which Sir John Harpur was obliged to pay to the Parliamentary government as a 'delinquent'. However, his estate remained intact and he survived the Commonwealth and Protectorate to die, a rich man, in 1679. His only son Henry had predeceased him, so, in accordance with a family settlement made in 1670, the entire Harpur estate passed to his cousin, Sir John Harpur of Calke.

Sir John was the grandson of that Henry Harpur for whom the Calke estate had been purchased in 1622. In 1625 Henry had held office as Sheriff of Derbyshire and in 1626 he purchased a baronetcy. Apart from this demonstration of social ambition, all we know of the first Harpur owner of Calke is that in 1624 the composer Francis Pilkington had dedicated to him his *Second Set of Madrigals and Pastorals*. Sir Henry died in 1639, leaving as his heir another John who, like his cousin of Swarkestone,

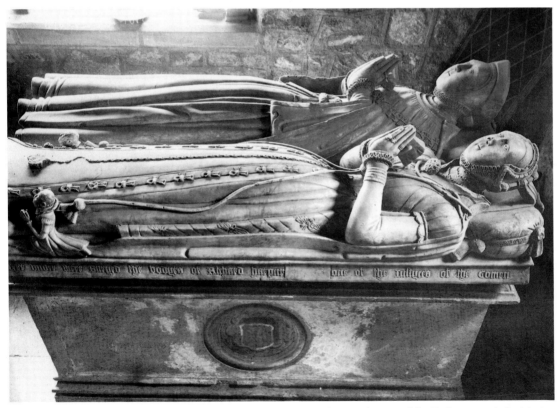

Richard Harpur, founder of the Harpur family fortunes, with his wife, Jane, heiress of the Finderns: on their alabaster tomb in Swarkestone Church by Richard and Gabriel Royley

had the difficult task of serving as Sheriff of Derbyshire in a critical year, 1641. Although his sympathies were Royalist, he played no significant part in the Civil War, and escaped denunciation as a 'delinquent'. Nevertheless, his record was suspect, and he was fined £578 18s 2d., the equivalent of one year's income. He lived to see the Restoration and died in 1669 aged 53. He was buried in Calke Church, where he was commemorated, not by a monument, but by a painted portrait showing him with his hand on a skull. In the nineteenth century this portrait was removed from the church in order to preserve it from damp and it is now to be seen hanging in the Saloon.

When, in 1679, the third Harpur owner of Calke inherited all his cousin's estates, Sir John was still a young man. But he lived to enjoy them for only two and half years before dying in August 1681, at the age of 36. He left two infant children, John, aged about fifteen months, and a daughter, Anne. Provided he survived the perils of childhood John

Sir John Harpur, 2nd Baronet, who died in 1669. This portrait (316), showing him with allusions to death and time, originally commemorated his burial in Calke Church but now hangs in the Saloon

would in due course inherit all the Harpur properties. In addition he would enjoy the accumulated income of a twenty years' minority. In 1701, when he entered into his inheritance, he had some £40,000 in hand, besides an annual income of between £2,000 and £3,000, equivalent to well over £100,000 in modern currency.

The previous owners of Calke had been established members of the Derbyshire gentry and they married the sons and daughters of other gentry: Bassets, Beaumonts, Gilberts, Lowes, Palmers, Pierreponts and Wilmots. By purchasing a baronetcy Henry Harpur had made a bid for a slightly higher status than his income could perhaps support. Now the entire Harpur inheritance came into the hands of his great-grandson, and a new and aristocratic social position was within his grasp. His marriage in 1702 increased both his status and his wealth. His wife, Catherine, was the daughter of a peer, Lord Crewe of Steane in Northamptonshire, and she brought with her a marriage portion of £12,000 besides a reversionary interest in part of the Crewe estate. Sir John proceeded immediately to rebuild his mansion at Calke, to purchase a house in London overlooking Green Park, and to acquire other symbols of aristocratic affluence such as fine silver, walnut furniture and damask hangings. But he showed no interest in public life. Though nominally a Tory, he left active participation in politics to the Curzons of Kedleston and to his cousin, John Harpur of Twyford, who was MP for Derby in 1701–2 and 1710. Sir John died suddenly at Calke in 1741, aged 61, and is commemorated by a handsome monument made by Henry Cheere in Calke Church.

Neither of the next two baronets shared Sir John's distaste for politics. Sir Henry, who died in 1748, represented first Worcester and then Tamworth, while Sir Harry, who died in 1789, was Member for the County of Derby from 1761 to 1768. But neither made any mark in the House of Commons, and both were better known as owners and breeders of racehorses than as public figures. With wives from Belvoir and Warwick castles they were members of the English aristocracy. Had they been more active politically they might have acquired a peerage to match their wealth and social

(*Above left*) Sir John Harpur, 4th Baronet, builder of Calke, attributed to Charles D'Agar (308; Saloon)

(*Above right*) Catherine Crewe, wife of Sir John Harpur, 4th Baronet, with one of her children by Charles Jervas (309; Saloon). This is probably the portrait referred to in the Calke accounts as 'May 1713, Pd Mr. Jervas for my Lady Harpur's picture £30'

status. As it was, the Harpurs were, in the words of the eighteenth-century county historian William Woolley, 'reckoned the best landed Family of any Commoners in this or any of the neighbouring Countys'.

Until the death of Sir Harry in 1789, the Harpurs of Calke had been notable only for their wealth. But the succession of his son Henry in that year marked the beginning of that congenital unsociability that was to be a characteristic of the family for two hundred years and which gives them a special place in the gallery of English eccentrics. In 1789 the new baronet was a young man of 25. When he had made the Grand Tour a few years earlier, his French tutor had remarked on an amount of knowledge unusual in a young Englishman of

his age, but also on an unhealthy taste for solitude. As soon as he became owner of Calke this shy young man withdrew from all the conventional contacts with society that were expected of a man in his position. 'My brother', his mother told a friend, 'thinks it a disgrace to his family and that he is lost to the world ... [and] never would be perswaded to mix in society and marry suitably ... He has no vices, and many good qualities, but will not be a man of the world.'

Not only did this eighteenth-century drop-out fail to fulfil his social obligations, he soon acquired a mistress – a lady's maid called Nanette Hawkins, with whom he lived in a small house in Calke Park before committing the ultimate impropriety of marrying her. Though her son's marriage came as a relief for his pious Evangelical mother in so far as it regulated an immoral relationship, to the world at large it was a *mésalliance* that was hardly mitigated by his refusal to allow 'any man, friend or servant to see his wife'. For the rest of his life the 'isolated baronet', as the headmaster of Repton School called him, lived at Calke in a self-imposed seclusion that in some respects resembled that of William Beck-

Sir Henry Harpur, 7th Baronet (50), and his wife Nanette Hawkins (58; both Drawing Room). The pastel portrait of Sir Henry, aged 21, was painted by the young Thomas Lawrence. Nanette married Sir Henry in 1792

ford at Fonthill. Though, unlike Beckford, he was not averse to hunting (in 1798 he bought Lord Moira's pack of hounds), he was fond of watching wild animals, and gave strict instructions that hares and pheasants that bred within sight of his windows were to be allowed to feed undisturbed by keepers, dogs and cats. He was, in fact, a man of sensibility, who devoted himself to the improvement of his house and the embellishment of his grounds. It was he who added the portico to the south front in 1806–8, who completed the landscaping of the park begun by his father, and who renamed his seat Calke Abbey. At Swarkestone he built an elegant classical 'Casina', long destroyed, from which to enjoy the views of the River Trent, and he remodelled the secondary family house at Repton Park in the Gothic style. In the summer he and his wife visited places like Aberystwyth, where the scenery was more interesting than the society, and from time to time he rented a country house in the Home Counties, from which they could make forays to the shops and exhibitions of London without incurring the social obligations of a regular London residence.

Sir Henry so far conformed to convention as to be, at least nominally, a JP and to serve reluctantly in 1794 as High Sheriff of Derbyshire. Patriotism induced him to raise a troup of Yeomanry from his estates during the Napoleonic Wars, and it was to provide his volunteers with appropriate music that in 1794 he commissioned Haydn to compose the *Derbyshire Marches* and had the music printed from plates that survive at Calke today. Sir Henry's social isolation did not prevent him from cherishing the idea of reviving the dormant barony of Crewe of Steane in his favour. Having hopefully changed his surname to 'Crewe' in 1808, he petitioned Crown and Prime Minister in vain for an honour which he had done nothing to earn either by public or political services.

The Yeomanry temporarily lifted Sir Henry out of his isolation and showed how his wealth and tastes might have been employed in a wider sphere had his temperament allowed it. As it was, once the emergency was over, this 'sad shy creature' withdrew once more from the world. In 1812 the artist and diarist Joseph Farington was given a vivid account of the 'singularities' of the owner of Calke by some Leicestershire acquaintances:

At dinner he sits down alone at a table covered for several persons, and after dinner glasses are placed as if for several persons and he takes wine in that form, but does not allow any servant to wait in the room . . . He keeps a pack of hounds, but does not himself hunt, yet . . . he has the pleasure in listening to his huntsman while he gives an account of each chase. His shyness is a disease of the mind, which he is sensible of but cannot conquer, and in letters to his friends he laments that he labours under this difficulty . . . He is shy of communication to such an excess that he sometimes delivers his orders to his servants *by letter*.

Some of these scribbled notes, mostly addressed to his Steward, survive.

Sir Henry Crewe was killed in a carriage accident in 1819, and was succeeded by his eldest son, George. In Sir George Crewe's lifetime the household at Calke was once more to be governed by the conventions of English upper-class life. An able and serious-minded man with a strong social conscience, he accepted his place in the life of the county and devoted himself to fulfilling his duties as a Christian landlord and a country gentleman. In 1835, at a time when the Tory interest in Derbyshire 'was apparently lost without hope of recovery', he

Sir George Crewe, 8th Baronet, with his son John, painted in 1828 by Ramsay Richard Reinagle (330)

was induced to stand for Parliament and won a notable victory at the polls. At Calke he was a meticulous and exacting squire who found much to put right after his father's idiosyncratic regime. He reformed the management of his estates, put the mansion into good repair, and in 1838 was able to record in his memorandum book that, 'under God's blessing, after 19 years labours . . . I have at last cleansed the Augean Stables of Calke jobs, Calke turkey and Calke extravagance'. Kitchen and cellar were brought under control and registers of every kind of consumption were instituted. As a landlord he had the reputation of being both just and generous, and devoted much time and money to the well-being of his poorer tenants.

In public life he was a man of strict principle who had no hesitation in doing whatever his conscience dictated, however contrary to established custom. Thus, he soon gave up hunting as a frivolous pursuit

Overpainted photograph of Sir John Harpur Crewe, 9th Baronet, executed in 1877 (618; Lobby)

which might take up too much of his time. In 1821, as Sheriff of the County, he discontinued the Assize Ball because he regarded it as unseemly for ladies and gentlemen to amuse themselves on the eve of the day on which others were to be tried for their lives, and in 1827 he refused to subscribe to a plate for the Derbyshire Yeomanry to race for because he considered that it would encourage betting.

Sir George was, however, neither a prig nor a puritan. He and Lady Crewe gave the County a handsome enough ball on another occasion, and most of the paintings by British and Netherlandish artists that hang at Calke were purchased by him. Never strong, he suffered from chronic bad health, and died suddenly in 1844 aged only 48.

In Sir George's son, Sir John Harpur Crewe, the symptoms of eccentricity reasserted themselves in modified form. At Calke he maintained his father's benevolent and paternal regime, but although he served his turn as High Sheriff of the county in 1853, when 'his long procession of tenantry, all mounted on good horses with new harness . . . made quite a sensation in the borough of Derby', he took no part in politics and was rarely seen outside his own property. At Calke there were few changes: more cases of stuffed birds and more cabinets of minerals were introduced to create that atmosphere of a private museum which Calke has retained to the present day. Little was done to alter the structure or to make provision for those house parties that were so characteristic of Victorian country-house life, for despite their great wealth, the Harpur Crewes rarely entertained. Lady Harpur Crewe's journal, covering the years 1853–65, records only two or three dinner parties of a modest character, and a Visitors' Book bought in the late nineteenth century was never used. Sir John, as his epitaph in the church records, 'was averse to a public life and spent the greater part of his days at Calke among his own people in the exercise of unostentatious charity and doing good to all around him'. As Sir John grew older he became more and more 'averse to a public life', devoting himself entirely to the management of his extensive estates, and in particular to the breeding of the longhorn cattle and Portland sheep for which Calke was celebrated in agricultural circles. Prizes won at agricultural shows were the only

Sir Vauncey Harpur Crewe, 10th and last Baronet, in his uniform as High Sheriff of Derbyshire, 1900

Little seen outside the bounds of Calke and Warslow, his secondary seat in Staffordshire, Sir Vauncey was a benevolent despot, combining great solicitude for his tenants and employees with a degree of aloofness towards his own family. Of the former an attractive picture is given in a letter written by a workman temporarily employed at Calke, in which he thanks Sir Vauncey 'for the great kindness' he had shown to him and his mate. 'If all the well-to-do', he concluded, 'were to treat those that work for them, as well as you do, there would not be that bitter feeling between the [upper] classes and the masses that there now is.' But to his children Sir Vauncey was a less benevolent figure, with whom relations were sometimes so strained that he would communicate with them only by letter, delivered by a footman on a silver salver, or even through the public post. To this son Richard he appears to have behaved well enough, allowing him

The children of Sir Vauncey and Isabel Harpur Crewe, photographed in about 1890: back row, Richard, Winifred and Airmyne; front row, Hilda and Frances. As Richard died young, Hilda inherited Calke Abbey on her father's death

public recognition which he sought, and it is said that on the increasingly rare occasions when he was away from home, the owner of 28,000 acres preferred a simple meal of bread and cheese in a public house to luncheon in a neighbouring country house.

Sir John Harpur Crewe died in 1886, after 42 years as the owner of Calke. He had married in 1845 his cousin Georgiana, daughter of Vice-Admiral William Stanhope Lovell, by Selina, daughter of his grandfather, Sir Henry Crewe. So their elder son, Vauncey, so named after a remote medieval ancestor called Sir Edmund Vauncey, was descended from Sir Henry on both sides, and in him the latter's idiosyncracies re-emerged. There was the same unsociability, the same arbitrary behaviour, the same 'shyness of communication'. Apart from serving as High Sheriff of Derbyshire in 1900, he played no part in public life. 'How completely he is losing or rather has lost all position in the County,' lamented his aunt Isabel in 1904. 'It vexes me terribly. I can't understand him. He does not seem to know how to behave like a Gentleman.'

Sir Vauncey's gamekeepers at Calke

sufficient means to indulge in his fondness for travel, ships, motoring, aeroplanes, photography and other manifestations of modern life that were rigidly excluded from the precincts of Calke. But to his daughters he was something of a tyrant. 'The Misses Crewe', he used to say, 'do not marry', and when they persisted in doing so, he was not pleased. As for Airmyne, the only daughter to oblige by remaining single, he turned her out of the house when he caught her breaking the ban on smoking which he imposed on all his household for fear of fire.

Having abdicated his social responsibilities, Sir Vauncey devoted himself almost entirely to birds and butterflies. From Sir Henry Crewe onwards, every owner of Calke had been something of an ornithologist. By 1840 there were already nearly 400 cases of stuffed birds, quadrupeds and fishes at Calke. But what for his predecessors had been a pastime became for Sir Vauncey an all-absorbing passion, upon which he regularly spent a substantial amount of money. Although he was a member of the British Ornithologists' Union and bought many books about birds and lepidoptera, his interest in these subjects was that of a collector rather than a scientist. At Calke he treated the park as a private bird sanctuary, neglecting its maintenance in every other respect. Even outside it, his agricultural tenants were forbidden to trim their hedges in the usual way in order to provide cover for nesting birds. He was never parted from his gun except on Sundays, when he left it in the porch of the church while attending morning service. His collection was not confined to birds that he had shot himself; he bought rare or abnormally coloured specimens from dealers and taxidermists. By the time of his death in 1924 the exhibits numbered several thousand and had invaded every floor of the house.

Had Richard Harpur Crewe lived to succeed his father, Calke might have come to terms with the twentieth century after Sir Vauncey's death, but his health was never good, and he predeceased his father, dying in 1921 at the age of 40. Three years later the estate passed to Sir Vauncey's eldest daughter Hilda, who had married Colonel Godfrey Mosley. To help to pay death duties the Mosleys sold off a quantity of stuffed birds, eggs and lepidoptera, as well as some of the most valuable books, such as Audubon's *Birds of America*.

In the autumn of 1940 the Mosleys welcomed ten

young evacuees to Calke, where they remained for nine months. School lessons were held in huts to the west of the house (until they were destroyed by fire), and the children slept in the servants' rooms on the first floor of the house. They were later joined by soldiers billeted in the stables, although the lack of electricity at Calke during Hilda's lifetime may explain why the army did not make more use of the house during the war.

When Hilda Mosley died in 1949 Calke went to her nephew, Charles Jenney, elder son of her younger sister, Francis. In Charles Harpur-Crewe (he changed his name in 1961, when he served as High Sheriff) the Harpur heredity asserted itself

once more. Unmarried, and more shy, retiring and socially isolated than any of his predecessors since Sir Henry, he made Calke for 32 years one of the two or three most impenetrable country houses in England. He consorted little with other Derbyshire landowners, preferring the company of tenant-farmers. Outside Calke he played a limited part in local life as an hereditary governor of Repton School, a member of the South Derbyshire District Council and as Chairman of the local Conservative Party. But he was notoriously silent at meetings and made little contribution to their deliberations. He died suddenly in March 1981, while setting mole-traps in the park.

Charles Harpur-Crewe, dressed as High Sheriff of Derbyshire in 1961, with his chaplain, the Rev. C. H. Cave, and his solicitor, J. R. S. Grimwood-Taylor

CHAPTER THREE
ARCHITECTURAL HISTORY

Standing deep in its park, Calke Abbey is revealed to the visitor only at the last moment. Its low-lying position in a hollow is a reminder of its monastic origin, for members of medieval religious orders liked secluded sites for their buildings. Standing in front of the house, the visitor sees a Baroque front of 1701–4 with the addition of a Greek Revival portico of 1806–8. A glance at the plan, however, reveals irregularities which must be due to the re-use of earlier foundations, and inside the central courtyard traces can be seen of the house as it existed prior to the great rebuilding of 1701–4.

The north side of the courtyard, showing the walled-up remains of the seventeenth-century arcaded loggia built up against one of the Elizabethan corner stairs turrets on the right

The earliest dateable masonry is Elizabethan. In the course of repairs in 1988 it was found that the lower part of an Elizabethan wall, with a characteristic moulded plinth, survives below the present ground level on the north side of the house, and other sections of plinth can be traced at various points inside and outside the house. In the courtyard the two re-entrant projections in the north-east and north-west corners can be interpreted as sixteenth-century stair-turrets. Built up against the two stair-turrets are the mutilated remains of an arcaded loggia of early seventeenth-century date. Only three arches now remain on either side, but originally they would almost certainly have returned across the south side of the courtyard. Although externally they have been deprived of nearly all their architectural detail, lozenge-shaped ornaments of early seventeenth-century character can still be seen carved on two of the arches on the east side.

If all the walls which offer evidence of sixteenth- or early seventeenth-century date are marked on a plan (p. 22), the outline of the house as it existed before 1701 emerges fairly clearly. It was evidently built round a courtyard, of which the north, east and west ranges partly survive within the present structure. There was probably a southern entrance front containing a gatehouse, the position of which may be indicated by the space between the two eighteenth-century staircases. The east and west ranges were not, however, quite parallel, and the east range was built of dressed stonework, while the west wing was of rubble. These discrepancies must reflect different phases of construction, and the alignment of the walls may well have been influenced by the priory buildings, some of which were probably still standing in the latter part of the sixteenth century.

Calke Abbey from the south-west

The Elizabethan rebuilding of Calke can be confidently attributed to Richard Wendsley, the first person in whom both the freehold and the leasehold interests in Calke were united since the dissolution of the priory. As mentioned earlier a contemporary document records that, having bought the property in 1575, he 'did build divers edifices thereupon and did inhabit and dwell upon the same'. Furthermore, witnesses giving evidence in 1640 said that Wendsley built a new parish church at Calke and that part of the manor house overlay the site of the old church. Robert Bainbridge, who owned Calke from 1585 to 1613, is not known to have done any building, and it is to the first Harpur owner of the house, Sir Henry, who died in 1639, that the loggia must be attributed. No plan survives of the house as it existed in the seventeenth century, but in 1662, when it was assessed for the Hearth Tax, it was found to contain 23 hearths, which made it one of the most substantial houses in the county, though

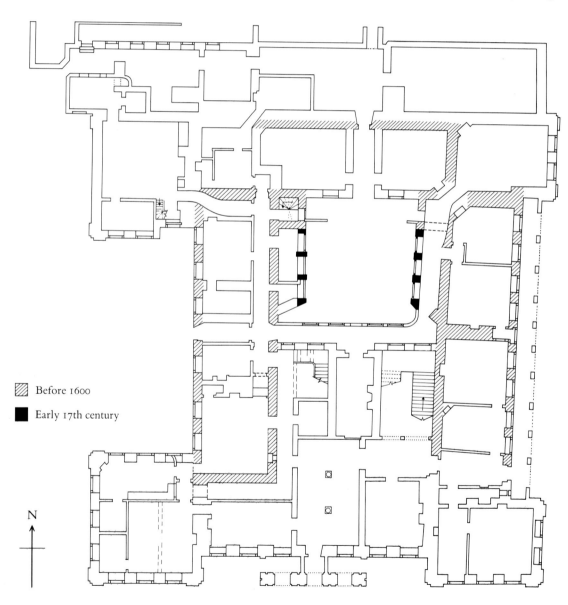

▨ Before 1600

■ Early 17th century

N

not quite as large as Swarkestone with 28 hearths, and far smaller than Hardwick (114), Chatsworth (79) or Bretby (68). Inventories of contents drawn up in 1639, 1670 and 1681 list the Hall, the 'Great Dining Chamber' or 'Dining Room', a smaller 'Dining Parlour', a Gallery, a Kitchen, and various other chambers and offices, including, in 1670, a 'Chapel Chamber' and a 'Gatehouse Chamber'. The position of the Hall is uncertain, but there are indications that, in the seventeenth century as in the eighteenth, the offices were in the west wing, while the living rooms were in the east wing.

Externally, however, all traces of the Elizabethan house were effectively disguised by rebuilding in 1701–4. Sir John Harpur's new mansion was of a grey sandstone from a quarry on his own land at Pistern Hill in the parish of Smisby, supplemented by some similar stone purchased from a quarry at Castle Donington. Bricks, lime, plaster and timber were all available on the estate, and lead for the roof and down-pipes was procured from mines in the Peak District. There were no general building contractors in the eighteenth century and, as was often the case when the owner was in a position to provide most of the materials himself, masons, carpenters, bricklayers and other building craftsmen were separately employed on a direct labour basis, piece- or task-work being reserved for specialised details. In the accounts the payments for building are mixed up with those for other purposes in a way which makes an exact calculation of the total cost impossible, but it was probably not less than £9,000. Between the spring of 1702 and the summer of 1704 some 60 masons were employed for varying periods, while two of them, named John Jordan and Simon Holt, were paid for unspecified task-work. The principal carpenters and joiners appear to have been men named Whelpdale and Leach. The carver was called Wright, the painter Reading, from Derby, and the plasterer Petty Dewick from Ashby-de-la-Zouch. The plumber, who was presumably responsible for the elaborately decorated downpipes and rainwater heads, was George Braseby.

No architect is mentioned, but in 1701 there were two payments to a 'surveyor' from Nottingham called Johnson, and in 1704 one of £5 to 'Mr Huitt Surveyor'. 'Surveyor' in contemporary parlance could mean either an architect or a land surveyor. The Johnson in question was almost certainly William Johnson who is known to have been in practice in Nottingham as an architect about this time. Huitt must have been a man of that name who was employed as a land-surveyor at nearby Melbourne Hall, and may have been the same as a French Protestant called 'Mr Huett' who was much involved in the supervision of both building and garden works at Chatsworth from 1694 to 1705. At Calke the single payment to Huitt just as the main house was finished is likely to have related to gardening rather than to architecture. Johnson, on the other hand, was presumably involved in the preparations for building the house, but without further evidence it would be unwise to conclude that he designed it.

In plan the house is a rectangular block with projecting corner pavilions. Such corner pavilions were a feature of country-house planning derived from France and were much favoured in England in about 1700. Ragley Hall in Warwickshire (1679), Tredegar Park in Monmouthshire (1674) and Hanbury Hall in Worcestershire (1701) are other examples of the type. Each pavilion was designed to contain on at least one of its floors an 'apartment' or set of rooms consisting of a bedroom, a private closet or study, and a room for a personal servant. There might also be a 'withdrawing room' or sitting room. In this way the occupant was provided with a suite of rooms similar to a self-contained modern flat, though without, of course, the amenities of running water and sanitation. At Calke such apartments originally existed in both the south-east and south-west pavilions, and still survive in an altered form on the ground and top floors.

Externally the pavilions are defined by fluted pilasters supporting a magnificently bold and elaborately decorated classical cornice. The capitals of these pilasters are of an unusual form and appear to be unique in English architecture. They are based on a capital seen among the ruins in Rome by the French architect Philibert de l'Orme and illustrated by him in his *Traité d'Architecture* published in Paris in 1567. De l'Orme's engraving was copied by another French architect, Julien Mauclerc, in a book published in Paris in 1648 and reprinted in London in 1669 as *A New Treatise of Architecture according to Vitruvius*. In de l'Orme's book the capital is classified as 'Composite', but Mauclerc labelled it as 'Ionic', and it is in fact a much enriched version of the Ionic order. It was no doubt from the English version of Mauclerc's book that the capital was selected as suitable for a building whose cornice demanded an ornate form of capital.

Inside the house, the central courtyard was retained, and the accommodation was arranged in three storeys: a high basement at ground-floor level, and two main floors, of which the upper was almost equal in height to the lower, and contained the principal bedrooms. This arrangement in a low-lying house had the advantage of giving the occupants better views into the park. As the roof was flat there were no attics and the servants' quarters were behind the state rooms on the first floor. On the south front most of the central block between the pavilions was occupied by a large hall, now the Saloon, approached internally by twin staircases at the back. On the east side was the Dining Room,

Detail of one of the capitals on the corner pavilions, derived from a plate in Philibert de l'Orme's treatise on architecture, 1567

now the Drawing Room, and on the west a smaller room, now the Breakfast Room, which in the 1740s was the 'Little Dining Parlour'. The present Dining Room in the south-west pavilion was originally subdivided to serve as an apartment, while the present Library was the Drawing Room.

Until 1728–9 there was apparently no external access to the Hall, but in those years a flight of stone stairs was built to designs by the London architect James Gibbs. It was later removed to make way for the present portico, but is seen in a painting of the south front, now in the Yale Center for British Art at New Haven, Connecticut, of which there is a nineteenth-century copy in the Breakfast Room at Calke.

Although externally the façade is symmetrical, the principal doorway at the top of the stone stairs (now behind the portico) was not in the middle bay of the Hall and at ground level the entrance doorway below was not centrally placed in relation to the twin staircases (see p. 22). This awkward relationship between exterior and interior was a consequence of the way in which the corner pavilions were set out. Whereas the south-west and north-west pavilions stand outside the west range of the house, the south-east and north-east ones are set within the width of the east range, from which they project only 5 feet. Had the south-east pavilion been

The stable block built by William Gilks for Sir John Harpur, 1712–14

sited to correspond to the south-west one, the recessed centre of the façade would have been two bays wider and the front doorway would have been on the central axis of the house, instead of some 10 feet to the west. Further architectural discrepancies are apparent in the re-entrant angle between the west wall and the north-west pavilion, and in adjustments made to the east front while it was under construction which left it with a centre awkwardly marked by two bays instead of one. How these discrepancies arose is difficult to understand, but it is clear that there was a certain amount of improvisation in the planning of the house, and an imperfect transcript exists of a lost letter in which someone who visited Calke while the work was in progress reported that Sir John Harpur was 'not well satisfied' with the design and had enquired whether someone could be found to 'sett the house in a better place'. The impression that it was designed without the best architectural advice is confirmed by a remark made in 1710 by Elizabeth Coke of Melbourne Hall to the effect that 'like Caulk House, the thing is done but nobody did it'.

In 1712–14 new stables completed Sir John Harpur's building programme. They form a substantial quadrangle, standing on the higher ground to the north west of the house, but partially concealed from it by trees. They were built by William Gilks, a local master-builder from Burton upon Trent, almost certainly to his own designs, and cost £1,250. Unlike the house, they are built of a mellow red brick with stone dressings, but like the house they are embellished with highly decorative rainwater heads bearing the Harpur crest of a boar. Above the entrance archway is an octagonal domed lantern surmounted by an iron weathervane. The latter, together with the decorative ironwork that supports it, was made by the celebrated Derby smith, Robert Bakewell, and was repaired and altered by him in 1750. Behind the stables is a second courtyard comprising more stable buildings, including a combined smithy and pigeon house.

Apart from the building of the stone stairs to the south front in 1728–9, no major alteration was made to the house until the end of the eighteenth century. An important addition was, however, made to the stable block in the form of a *manège* or riding school. This was built in 1768 to the designs of the Derby architect Joseph Pickford. It is a large plain brick building with a viewing gallery at one end. The roof is supported by immense wooden trusses of a kind illustrated in Francis Price's *British Carpenter*, the leading manual of Georgian structural carpentry.

Surviving designs for an entirely new house, probably made by Joseph Pickford, are evidence

Painting of the south front of the house, with the stone stairs designed by James Gibbs and built 1728–9. On the coach are the arms of Sir Henry Harpur, 5th Baronet, thus dating the picture to the 1740s (Yale Center for British Art, New Haven)

that Sir Harry Harpur was not entirely satisfied with his vast and somewhat awkwardly planned mansion, but it was his son, the 'isolated baronet', who between 1789 and 1810 transformed the house both inside and out. His architect, William Wilkins the Elder (father of the William Wilkins who designed the National Gallery in London), had recently designed nearby Donington Park for Lord Moira. Donington was an essay in the Gothic Revival, but at Calke all Wilkins's work was classical in style. Under his direction the entrance front was transformed by the substitution of a Greek Revival portico with Ionic columns based on those of the Erechtheum at Athens for the stone steps designed by Gibbs. In order not to darken the ground-floor rooms, access to the Hall or Saloon doorway was by means of flights of steps on either side of the portico. Always rather flimsy in appearance, these were removed in the 1930s, thus finally depriving the Saloon of its original function as a formal entrance hall. On the east side of the house Wilkins built a long balcony at first-floor level to provide attractive views of the garden. Another important alteration of these years was the erection

of the stone balustrade round the top of the house. Although work on a parapet was begun in 1709, it had never been finished, and the painting at Yale shows the house without a parapet of any kind. In the park Wilkins designed three lodges, including the Middle Lodge, notable for the bold scale of its neo-Classical archway.

Inside the house the principal rooms were re-arranged. The apartment at first-floor level in the south-west pavilion was cleared away to make way for a spacious new Dining Room. The existing Dining Room in the south-east pavilion became the Drawing Room, while the old Drawing Room was enlarged to form a Library. Wilkins's neo-Classical decoration survives unaltered in the Dining Room, and the Library remains essentially as he designed it, with the bookshelves canted at each end to give visual interest. It was also at this time that the Kitchen, hitherto in the west wing, was removed to its present position in the north-west pavilion.

When Sir George Crewe succeeded his father in 1819 his first architectural enterprise was, predictably for a man noted for his piety, to rebuild the church in the park, and it was not until 1840 that

The south and east fronts at Calke from a photograph taken in 1886. Sir John Harpur Crewe's funerary hatchment can be seen on the pediment to the portico. The stairs flanking the portico were dismantled in the 1930s

The Saloon, showing the wall built by Henry Isaac Stevens for Sir John Harpur Crewe in 1841, with the family portraits hung on panels above the mid-cornice

he turned his attention to the house. A thorough architectural overhaul ensued under the direction of the Derby architect Henry Isaac Stevens. On the ground floor the present Entrance Hall was formed by combining two existing rooms, and the left-hand of the two staircases was rebuilt in stone and cut off from the Entrance Hall, the better to perform its function as a back stair. Upstairs, the Saloon was remodelled. Before 1841 it was askew at the east end because it followed the alignment of an ancient wall which had not been at right angles to the front of the house. Stevens straightened out this end of the room, providing a new chimney-piece, but merely adjusting the pilasters and broken pediment that frame it. Above the level of the cornice

he divided the wall up into panels to provide space for family portraits, and he remodelled the ceiling with recessed compartments displaying the family crest between finely moulded bands of ornament.

Since 1841–2 there have been no significant alterations to the fabric of Calke Abbey. In 1865–6 Henry Marley Burton carried out a number of minor repairs and improvements, but his proposals for corridors round the courtyard and other major alterations found no favour with Sir John Harpur Crewe and, apart from the introduction of the telephone in 1928 and of electricity in 1962, no subsequent owner of Calke has even contemplated modernising the house. Although some maintenance has been carried out by the estate, by the time the house passed into the hands of the National Trust in 1985 it was in a poor state and in 1986–8 extensive repairs were carried out under the direction of Rodney Melville.

CHAPTER FOUR

THE CONTENTS OF THE HOUSE

As the fate of Calke Abbey hung in the balance in the early 1980s, the house and its contents were saved by a spirited publicity campaign that brought about financial rescue, as detailed in the next chapter. What made Calke Abbey so special, indeed so peculiar, and what fascinated so many people was its contents. Photographs in magazines and newspapers showed the clutter of Sir Vauncey's bedroom, of case upon case of stuffed birds and animals in the Saloon, and of the State Bed emerging from its chrysalis of boxes in the Linen Closet.

The contents of Calke reflect the interests, qualities and peculiarities of the Harpur family. Some of the collections were formed gradually and by chance; others were created obsessively over a period of sustained activity. The collection of paintings at Calke comes in the first category; never great aesthetes, the Harpurs acquired paintings that reflected their interests, first in establishing the family's place in society, and then in their horses and prize farm animals. The natural history collections, mainly the work of Sir John Harpur Crewe and of Sir Vauncey, come into the second category, and dominate the contents of the house. The remarkable collection of carriages in the stableyard are a reflection of Sir Vauncey's desire for seclusion and the banning of motor traffic from the park in the 1920s.

Finally, there is the great accumulation of all manner of objects at Calke that so particularly stamped the character of the house. In the nineteenth century the Harpur Crewes developed a tendency never to throw anything away. This tendency reached a peak in Sir Vauncey's time, so that today the visitor can see evidence of the life of a late Victorian household as if caught by the photographer's lens.

THE PICTURES

Considering that in the eighteenth century the Harpurs were one of the richest families in Derbyshire, it is remarkable that they did not amass a more impressive picture collection, particularly as the 5th, 6th and 7th baronets all made the Grand Tour. In the eighteenth century the Grand Tour provided the starting point for many of the great English country-house collections, but the only evidence of a picture deriving from Harpur continental expeditions appears in a list of Calke paintings drawn up by Isabel Crewe in 1883. Here she refers to a Madonna and Child copied from the Raphael in Naples by Sir Henry Harpur's valet, hardly a major addition to the collection.

This, moreover, sets the tone for the rest of the collection. No member of the Harpur family seems to have had great aesthetic sensibility, nor any particular knowledge of painting. The *raison d'etre* for most of the paintings is that they related to Calke Abbey and Park, and their inhabitants. A large number of pictures are family portraits, starting in the late seventeenth century and acquired for prestige rather than artistic considerations. Throughout the following century, the major acquisitions were portraits. Sir John Harpur, the 4th Baronet, not only built himself a splendid new house but spent lavishly on furnishings, silver and paintings. He commissioned several portraits of his immediate family, including the two double portraits at the top of the stairs showing four of his children, Henry and John by Charles D'Agar and Edward and Catherine by John Verelst.

Sir Henry, the 5th Baronet, established a good connection by marrying Lady Caroline Manners, daughter of the 2nd Duke of Rutland, and did not hesitate to advertise the fact on the walls of Calke, with portraits of Lady Caroline's brother, the 3rd Duke with his Duchess, and her sister, the Duchess

The bedroom that Sir Vauncey Harpur Crewe occupied as a young man. This photograph was taken in 1984 when Calke's plight was first revealed and epitomises the accumulation of contents in the house and outbuildings

of Montrose. Another prestigious union followed with the marriage of Sir Harry, the 6th Baronet, to Lady Frances Greville, daughter of the 1st Earl of Warwick. As a result his Greville relatives appear in a number of portraits in the Drawing Room, while the magnificent picture by Tilly Kettle of Lady Frances and her son Henry dominates the Saloon.

Sir Harry also started the great collection of animal portraits at Calke. His grandfather had no sooner finished rebuilding the house than he turned his attention to the stables built between 1712 and 1716. Sir Harry began to record his victories on the turf with portraits of four of his most successful racehorses, painted in 1774.

In fact, Sir Harry displayed greater artistic perception than the rest of his family. *En route* to Bath with his family, he stopped at the Bear Hotel in Devizes to change horses and was impressed by the talents of Thomas Lawrence, the fifteen-year-old son of the innkeeper. Pastel portraits of Sir

29

Harry and his son Henry by the young Lawrence hang in the Drawing Room, and Sir Harry offered to pay for the boy to study painting in Italy, an offer which Lawrence Senior refused.

Sir Harry's grandson, Sir George Crewe, must have inherited some of his grandfather's acumen. He was responsible for collecting the largest number of pictures, including some good English works, such as the Lely portrait in the Breakfast Room, and paintings by nineteenth-century artists such as Linnell, Etty and John Ferneley Senior. He also collected Old Masters, mostly Dutch genre scenes by lesser artists.

During the nineteenth century some pictures were commissioned from local artists like Ferneley,

Thomas Lawrence's pastel portrait of Sir Harry, the 6th Baronet (49; Drawing Room). Impressed by the young artist's talents, Sir Harry wanted to become his patron

but more were bought from local dealers and surviving documents range from a request for payment of five guineas for two drawings by Henry Moore of Derby in 1808 to a receipt for £20 for a portrait from W. Windle, a Nottinghamshire dealer, in 1888. Most were purchased for modest prices.

Sir George, however, often bought wisely. The Landseer *Greyhounds Resting* was acquired at the British Institution in 1823, and a letter of 1829 from Sir Thomas Lawrence to Sir George makes clear that Lawrence was buying paintings and drawings for him. Once more it was an equestrian subject, acquired from Christie's, a painting by James Ward that has subsequently disappeared: 'I perceive that one clever picture has been procured for you – one, I think of his very best – the study of an aged horse – but not so old as to present an offensive form'.

Sir John Harpur Crewe combined the family interest in horses with a passion for agriculture, so

Tilly Kettle's portrait of Lady Frances, wife of the 6th Baronet, with her son Henry, destined to become the 'isolated baronet' (317; Saloon)

paintings of cattle and sheep joined the Calke collection. He bought several works by John Ferneley, including the large and important *Council of Horses* now on the Staircase. Sir John's local commitments prompted him to lend fifteen paintings and some silver to the 1870 Midland Counties Exhibition in Derby, probably the last time that any of the Calke contents were seen by the public until the Tilly Kettle portrait was lent to the Royal Academy in 1956–7.

Although Sir John's heir, Sir Vauncey, paid 300 guineas for a Great Auk's egg in 1894, he was not interested in picture buying, and the only paintings

recorded as entering the collection in his lifetime were three portraits, two of the family, and a painting of the Abbey by John Glover Junior. At Sir Vauncey's death in 1924, large death duties were levied and Christie's made a valuation of the Calke pictures. Luckily there were no works of great worth; a few were offered at Christie's in 1929, remained unsold and returned to the house. Despite the disappearance of one or two pictures – the worst loss being a view of Elizabethan Calke recorded in 1748 – the collection has remained intact and is still hung very much as Sir John Harpur Crewe organised it over a hundred years ago.

John Ferneley's masterpiece, *The Council of Horses*, which hangs on the principal staircase (86)

THE NATURAL HISTORY COLLECTIONS

The natural history collections at Calke are remarkable for their range and diversity, and for the degree to which they have survived intact. The range is prodigious: major representations in the fields of entomology, oology, conchology, botany, geology and palaeontology. In addition, there is a huge collection of taxidermy, particularly of bird and mammal specimens, but also of fish and reptiles, preserved nests and skeletons.

Although the collections are largely the work of the last two baronets, Sir John and Sir Vauncey Harpur Crewe, Sir Henry Crewe, the 'isolated baronet', was deeply interested in natural history. As mentioned earlier, one of his favourite pastimes was watching the wild animals in his park, and his accounts include payments for the 'setting up' of bird specimens.

This family interest continued, so that by 1840 there were nearly 400 cases of stuffed birds and other vertebrates at Calke. Most of these were acquired by Sir John, and he too compiled the geological, fossil and conchological specimens which are displayed in the Saloon, where they are arranged to look well rather than organised systematically. However, in other rooms at Calke the collection takes a more ordered form, and the whole reveals a keen and informed amateur interest in the subject. There is a broad coverage of mineral types and rock

Stuffed birds and animals from Sir Vauncey's collection in glass-fronted cabinets in the Saloon

One of the glazed cabinets in the Saloon with some of the fossils and beach detritus collected by Sir John Harpur Crewe

samples, many of which have been expertly polished, and there are numerous fine examples of crystal formations. The palaeontological material is less extensive, but includes a number of exceptional fossil fish. Sir John's conchological collection comprises mainly the tropical marine shells on view in the Saloon, and he also appears to have been responsible for the smaller collections of shells, snails, small fossils, beach detritus and other curiosities elsewhere in the house.

The preoccupation with natural history reached its zenith in the last Baronet, Sir Vauncey. His collections follow a more scientific pattern, mostly contained in museum-type storage rather than in display cabinets, so that much of it is hidden from view, and is likely to remain so for some time.

Sir Vauncey's collections fall into five main categories: entomological (insects), oological (birds' eggs), herbaria (plants), conchological (shells) and taxidermy. Perhaps the most important of these is the insect collection, comprising around 10,000 specimens of British butterflies and moths. Originally the collection was much larger: many of the lepidoptera were sold to meet taxes following the death of Sir Vauncey, together with many of the eggs and stuffed birds. Pests have taken their toll, so that the remaining material represents probably less than half the original. Even so, the collection contains many rarities, collected by Sir Vauncey, acquired by exchange with entomological friends, or purchased from dealers. Two of Sir Vauncey's captures are illustrated in F. W. Frohawk's classic *Varieties of British Butterflies*, published in 1938, and some of his purchased specimens appeared in earlier texts. In addition to the butterflies and moths, the collection contains several hundred specimens of British beetles, flies, bees and wasps.

The egg collection now comprises about 1,500 birds' eggs, again the residue of a much larger collection. Sir Vauncey purchased many eggs at auc-

Part of Sir Vauncey Harpur Crewe's collection of butterflies, moths and birds' eggs

tion or from dealers, including several rare items such as the celebrated Great Auk's egg, for which he paid 300 guineas in 1894, but which was sold after his death. Most of those that remain have little or nothing in the way of identifying marks, and so their scientific value is probably slight. However, the eggs are well preserved and their value may be enhanced by study of records relating to their acquisition.

The Calke herbaria comprise separate collections of higher plants, mosses, lichens and fungi, all British and numbering several thousand specimens. Part of the collection belonging to the Rev. Andrew Bloxham, a master at Rugby School and a specialist on brambles, wild roses and fungi, was absorbed into the Calke collection. The specimens are mounted on herbarium sheets and stored in boxes or in stacks of folders.

Sir Vauncey's conchological collection, unlike his father's, is composed mainly of examples of British freshwater and terrestrial species, stored in

a fairly orderly fashion in a beautiful glass-fronted cabinet which stands in Sir Vauncey's bedroom.

Evidence of Sir Vauncey's enthusiasm for taxidermy is everywhere apparent to the visitor to Calke: his collection is one of the country's largest in private ownership, and one of the least known as he was so unwilling to show it. Rarely seen without his gun at his shoulder, Sir Vauncey would set off on shooting expeditions with his head gamekeeper, Agathos Pegg, and many of the specimens in the collection are the result of these forays. Others he purchased from various sources, often spending large sums of money. These generous payments were a temptation to dealers, and although many of the specimens that were bought were described as 'British killed', they were probably obtained abroad.

Sir Vauncey in typical pose with gun over his shoulder. Copies of this photograph were given to his tenants after his death in 1924

The specimens were mounted in display cases. Some were organised by Sir Vauncey himself with the help of Pegg: some of the bird skins in various stages of preparation were found hanging in one of the bedrooms at Calke when the National Trust took over the house. Woe betide any servant who failed to keep the fires burning to maintain an even temperature in the cases. Too hot a fire resulted in instant dismissal, but as Sir Vauncey couldn't tell one servant from another, the victim generally survived the sacking.

Other specimens, often in specially prepared diorama cases, were produced for Sir Vauncey by commercial taxidermists, notably Thomas Gunn and his son Frederick of Norwich. Examples of Thomas's skill at Calke include cases of Bewick's and whooper swans, capercaillie and a spectacular family of great bustards. In the Saloon are several good displays of mammals: four adult foxes with two cubs, four otters, badgers, red squirrels, stoats and weasels.

The reclusive master of Calke was fascinated by hybrids, freaks and colour varieties. Among these bizarre exhibits are white and partly white blackbirds, all-white lapwings, robins, house martins and jackdaws, while Frederick Gunn produced a series of watercolours also showing birds in freak plumage. The last record of this strange interest came after Sir Vauncey's death, when part of the vast collection was put up for sale and the auction catalogue drew particular attention to the 'unique and remarkable varieties ... albinos, melanistic, pied ... also a large number of hybrids, chiefly of game birds'.

THE CARRIAGES

The carriages at Calke Abbey form a fascinating collection. Some are very fine and it is remarkable to find examples of so many different types still in the place for which they were originally built, giving an insight into the way carriages were used at the turn of the century.

It is also interesting to find that the Harpur Crewe family patronised a local coachbuilder. Many of the important landed families bought their carriages from one of the famous London builders, but at Calke there was no need to consider this. H. and A. Holmes, later Holmes and Co. of London Road,

Derby, were a prominent and successful firm. They had showrooms in London, Sheffield, Lichfield and Burton upon Trent, as well as their head office, works and showroom in Derby. Two family members became Masters of the Worshipful Company of Coachmakers and Coach Harness Makers. Few provincial coachbuilders achieved comparable fame and status.

The existence of the collection today is, no doubt, largely due to the reluctance of Sir Vauncey Harpur Crewe to accept the advances of the twentieth cen-

tury. While most houses were discarding their carriages and replacing them with cars, he refused to allow cars in the park right up to his death in 1924. Guests were obliged to leave cars at the Ticknall Lodge and wait for a carriage, complete with rugs and refreshments, to bring them to the house. Some must have found this infuriating, but we should be grateful to him.

The finest carriages in the collection – the brougham, victoria and landau – are examples of the three types of coachman-driven carriages in most general use from the middle of the last century until the end of the carriage age. They were all built by Holmes at the end of the century.

The first brougham was built in 1839 and, for the next sixty years or so, this type of carriage was developed, refined and produced in vast numbers. They could have single bodies to seat two, double bodies for four, square or round fronts, angular or rounded profiles. The brougham at Calke is a square-fronted double brougham with angular profile. Its fixed splinter bar shows that it was always driven to a pair of horses. It has a basket which can be fitted to the roof to carry luggage.

The victoria was a development of the earlier George IV phaetons, with the addition of a box seat.

(*Above*) Detail from one of the Calke carriages showing the label of Holmes & Co. of Derby, distinguished coachbuilders and suppliers of many of the vehicles at Calke

(*Right*) Square-fronted double brougham built by Holmes of Derby in about 1890

It was contemporary with the brougham and, like it, built in many different forms. The pretty victoria at Calke has a panel boot and a cut-under body with concave back panel. Although it generally carried two passengers in the comfortable body, there is a little folding seat to enable one or two more to be carried occasionally. It is light enough to be used with one horse, and has no provision for a pair.

Landaus date from the first half of the eighteenth century, and accounts at Calke show that there was one here in 1742, but it was not until about a hundred years later, when more people became carriage owners and smaller carriages were in general use, that landaus became so popular and widely used. The landau at Calke is a Sefton, or canoe-bodied, landau and could be used with a single horse or a pair.

Carriages of these types were owned by professional and middle-class people but they were also the everyday carriages of the wealthy and titled, who could use more ostentatious carriages for important social occasions. The accounts from Holmes show that there was a coach and a chariot, a two-seat version of a coach, at Calke until about 1860, and a barouche until about 1900.

The other carriages are all owner-driven varieties, which shows that some members of the family must have enjoyed driving themselves.

The two large phaetons would have been driven by a gentleman for social calls, family outings and for attending sporting events. One is definitely by Holmes, and the other is attributed to them. The smaller is an interesting and unusual carriage because, by changing the arrangement of the seating in the back of the body, it can become three different carriages: with the seat facing forward it is a Stanhope phaeton; with it facing backwards and the tail-board lowered, it is a four-wheeled dog cart; and with two seats mounted longitudinally and facing inwards it becomes a wagonette, with access through the little central door. The larger, a handsome Stanhope phaeton, has two poles, one of which is suitable for a team of four horses, implying that at least one member of the family was a keen coachman, because a pair of horses would be quite adequate for this carriage.

The four-wheeled ralli car would have been used

in a similar way to the phaetons, but it is a little further down the social scale, being suitable for informal occasions, with a single cob or a pair of ponies.

The governess cart is what its name implies and would have been used by the governess, or sometimes the mother, to take the children for a drive. It has a safe deep body and long splash boards (mudguards) fitted right up to the body, possibly to prevent children from getting their hands dirty, or even hurt, by touching the wheels.

The pretty vis-à-vis phaeton, of very angular form, would have been used by a lady to take a friend for a drive or possibly to make short-distance social calls.

The varnished float is a little informal two-wheeler, and very possibly came from the home farm or one of the other houses on the estate. It is unlikely that anyone from the big house would have used it.

Calke's eighteenth-century hand-pump fire engine, buried in clutter in the stableyard

The estate's own hand-pump fire engine is an early example of a Newsham type, probably built in the second quarter of the eighteenth century. It has its own transporting waggon, with a fitted windlass to haul it up the ramps. There is also a wheeled Shand Mason twin-cylinder fire pump of much later date and two Shand Mason telescopic fire escapes, one extending to 45 feet and the other to 30 feet high, both supplied in 1889.

The collection is completed by a bath chair which would have been pushed by a servant while the occupant steered with a tiller; a little children's goat cart with an attractive carriage character; and a hand bier used for transporting coffins short distances, which comes from the church.

In addition to the carriages themselves, several pairs of lamps have survived, as well as a quantity of driving harness, including a lovely little set for the goat carriage, all in remarkably good condition.

MISCELLANEA

In addition to the easily categorised collections, the interest of Calke is enhanced by what might be described as a collection by default, the extraordinary accumulation of contents reflecting every aspect of life, high and low. Sadly, very little survives of the sumptuous furnishings – silver, walnut furniture, damask hangings – introduced into his new house by Sir John Harpur in 1704. Instead, when the National Trust came to take over Calke, public imagination was caught by the idea that here was a house where 'nothing had been thrown away', where the pulse of life in Victorian and Edwardian times still beat, albeit faintly.

Inevitably this aspect was exaggerated in the press and television coverage of the saving of Calke. Some of the picturesque disarray photographed in back rooms of the house was caused by clearance for the army in the last war, some arose as the neighbouring rooms were cleared in the battle against dry rot, and some was the work of the auctioneer's valuers. Exaggerated or not, the clutter that crowded so many of the rooms represented an extraordinary archaeological deposit to be explored and catalogued. As this was done, so the nineteenth-century life of the household was illuminated in vivid and fascinating detail.

Some of the treasures discovered in the Schoolroom: Victorian dolls found undisturbed in drawers

Of great appeal were the things associated with childhood. The doll's house and rocking horse still stood in the Schoolroom, but the excitement of discovery began when drawers revealed hordes of dolls, carefully wrapped, sets of lead soldiers in mint condition in their boxes, quantities of children's books and games, two green tin trams on a wooden track, and twenty miniature chairs. In the Cook's Room, an isolated eyrie up a narrow staircase from the Kitchen, were found in wooden trunks hundreds of late nineteenth-century children's nightdresses, cotton smocks, baby clothes, sailor suits and other outfits.

The room occupied by Sir Vauncey in his boyhood and youth was one of the most crowded, containing not only the butterflies and birds' eggs already discussed, but also hundreds of trinkets and souvenirs, from an amber monkey to a miniature

silver-gilt scent bottle in the form of a ship, a large collection of purses in bead, leather and fur, and a huge quantity of walking sticks. Notes and labels written by Sir Vauncey and addressed to himself, like 'this cupboard was dusted in 1921 and will not need dusting again until 1924', reflect the private nature of the collector's obsession, creating a neatly ordered world under his exclusive control.

Some things were found in a state of romantic decay, such as the mid-eighteenth-century sedan chair in the stables, or the remains of the chairs bought for the Saloon by Sir Henry from Marsh & Tatham, abandoned in the disused scullery.

One treasure of national importance that was

unearthed was the great early eighteenth-century Chinese silk state bed, wrapped up in boxes in the Linen Closet (see p.69). Among other textiles were beautifully embroidered eighteenth-century waistcoats and dress coats, a bundle labelled 'Sir Harry's stockings', the blue uniforms of Sir Henry's Derbyshire Yeomanry, and large numbers of Victorian and Edwardian dresses.

Although much has still to be discovered about the musical interests of the family, apart from Sir Henry's commission from Haydn, several instruments came to light. The star was a harpsichord by the great maker Burkhardt Shudi. This lay under a thick layer of dust, abandoned in a loft above the stables. Other instruments include an eighteenth-century chamber organ, a Regency chamber barrel-organ, grand pianos by Broadwood and Erard, an eighteenth-century mandolin and guitar and some very uncommon nineteenth-century instruments – a *sticcado pastorale* percussion crystallaphone and a flutina.

The more important objects are described in Chapter Six. More will be put on show as the rooms in the east range of the house are gradually opened to visitors. At the same time, museum displays, with regularly changed contents, will be set up in the rooms beyond the state bed museum, so that visitors can see selections of objects from the items that make up the unique inventory of Calke.

(*Above*) Close-up of the keyboard and signature of the 1821 Mott piano, rescued from a loft in the stables

(*Right*) Chairs from the set of 24 made by Marsh & Tatham in 1806–7 for the Saloon, as they were found in 1983 in the Scullery

(*Left*) The doll's house in the Schoolroom

CHAPTER FIVE
THE RESCUE OF CALKE

When Charles Harpur-Crewe died in 1981, he had made no arrangements to protect the estate from death duties. As a result, his younger brother, Henry, was saddled with a tax bill of £8 million, which at the end of a period of grace began to attract interest charges amounting to £1,500 per day. There seemed to be nothing for it but to sell up and watch 400 years of family history disappear.

It was Henry Harpur-Crewe's determination to preserve Calke intact that led to its rescue. At his request, the house, contents and almost all the estate, up to the value of the tax owed, were offered to the Treasury in the hope that they could be passed over to the care of the National Trust, and that the estate would provide the necessary funds for repair and maintenance. The total value of the Calke estate was £14 million, and thus the resources were there, so long as the Treasury would agree to divert the funds from the taxman's purse. The setback came when the Treasury agreed to accept the house, contents and park, but refused the 'non-heritage' land that would support them.

An intensive publicity campaign was then mounted by Save Britain's Heritage in aid of Calke. Henry Harpur-Crewe allowed himself to be photographed amid the amazing clutter of his family home, and to be interviewed for television and the press on Calke's plight. The National Heritage Memorial Fund, the Historic Buildings Council (now English Heritage), the All-Party Heritage Group of MPs, the South Derbyshire District Council and other local authorities and the National Trust also moved into action, all urging the Government to think again.

By 1984, with interest charges still mounting, it was obvious that time was running out. The National Heritage Memorial Fund, taking the initiative, brought together all the interests concerned: the National Trust, with the help of an anonymous benefactor, and a commitment to appeal to the public for £250,000, undertook to contribute £1 million; the Harpur-Crewe Trustees undertook to match the Trust's £1 million; the Historic Buildings Council committed £1 million in repair grants; and the Department of the Environment agreed to redefine the area of the 'heritage' land. But the shortfall still remained. Calke's salvation came dramatically and unprecedentedly in the Budget speech of the Chancellor of the Exchequer, Nigel Lawson, on 13 March, when he announced he would provide the National Heritage Memorial Fund with £4.5 million to save the house and park. The day was won.

Henry Harpur-Crewe in the bedroom of his grandfather, Sir Vauncey: part of the press campaign that brought the plight of Calke to public attention

Once the money was assured, and Calke Abbey passed to the care of the National Trust, so the physical work of rescue could begin. An enormous amount of building work was needed to repair the structure and provide a heating system to prevent dampness, safe electrical wiring, and alarms against fire and theft. But first, all those contents that had captured the imagination of the outside world had to be packed up and removed. Each room was photographed as it was, then every object was numbered, photographed and catalogued, from the State Bed to a housemaid's broken candlestick. Woodworm in the furniture and moth, beetle and mildew in textiles, books and stuffed birds were treated. Then all these precious objects were transferred to Sir Harry's great Riding School, with economically arranged humidity control.

One of Calke's great architectural splendours is its massive overhanging stone cornice. But rusting iron internal reinforcements were splitting the stone, causing the splendour to turn into a menace,

(*Above left*) Gilbert Cooper, one of the skilled plumbers who produced new rainwater heads for Calke. Each new head carried the Harpur crest of the boar, the date of the old rainwater head and the year of its remaking

as fragments periodically crashed to the ground. The cornice was dismantled and each stone assessed to decide whether it had to be replaced. Once the replacements were up, the masons copied the carved ornaments onto them, but to avoid mechanical repetition of a single model, they made use of detailed photographs. Nearly three centuries earlier their predecessors used models from pattern books, otherwise their methods were identical.

Inside the house, great pains were taken to avoid damage to surfaces of walls, woodwork, floors and ceilings in the course of structural investigation and installing wires and pipes. Where walls were covered by wallpaper, skilled conservators could remove the paper and put it back after necessary work had been undertaken. Concern for old surfaces even extended to parts of the house not likely to be seen by visitors, such as the family and servants' rooms in the north range that are destined to be storerooms.

At the conclusion of most large repair projects redecoration is inevitable, but to do so at Calke would destroy the particular quality of the house. Only two rooms, therefore, were redecorated: the Caricature Room and the Dining Room, where important historical schemes had recently been covered up.

Calke's contents were treated in the same way so that they should not look new and thus stand out when returned to the rooms. Canvases of paintings were restretched and secured, but apart from essential cases, they were not cleaned by the removal of layers of varnish. Furniture was made sound, but

The wine cellar in the final stages of decay

not over-polished or restored to perfection. The faded and tattered chintz case covers in the Library and Drawing Room were painstakingly reinforced by methods normally reserved for much more precious and vulnerable textiles.

Possibly the most challenging task of all was the reweaving of the Drawing Room curtains. Warner Fabrics found the design in their own archive. Richard Humphries was then commissioned to weave the new curtains on his hand-looms. These were made of a luxurious yellow silk tissue, originally woven by ex-Spitalfields weavers under royal patronage in 1857. By 1985 the effect of light had reduced them in parts to powder. To reproduce the pattern, every intersection of the warp and weft was noted on graph paper extending to over 1 million squares. The design then required 12,500 punched Jacquard cards to marshal the raising and lowering of the loom and to control 9,600 glass eyelets through which the warps were threaded in correct sequence, without margin for a single error.

Howard Colvin, the architectural historian, had been a friend of Henry Harpur-Crewe since 1964. With Joan Sinar, the County Archivist for Derbyshire, he undertook the task of retrieving family papers from different parts of the house. One important bundle of architectural drawings was rescued from a cavity behind bookshelves in the Library with the aid of a fishing rod.

The building repair works enabled a thorough archaeological survey to be carried out. When work was taking place on a part of the north wall of the house, below ground level, the bases of late sixteenth-century, three-light mullioned windows, doors and plinths in a good state of preservation were uncovered, confirming the Elizabethan origins of the house. Remains of what may be assumed to be buildings of the Priory were revealed by trenches on the east side of the house, and a fine, twelfth-century carved capital was found under a floor. Five adult male skeletons in different forms of burial were also uncovered. They date from the twelfth to fourteenth centuries, and the fact that they were laid to rest in a strict east-west axis suggests that they are the remains of monastic occupants of Calke. Their bodies are now reinterred in the churchyard.

Rescue work has also gone on in the park and gardens at Calke. In the pleasure grounds new plantings are making good the depredations of the deer, moved here twenty years ago when the Staunton Harold reservoir was built. Now the deer are safely accommodated in the park. In the kitchen and flower gardens the gardener and his staff are bringing neatness and order to their domain.

Even after years of intensive work on the buildings, grounds and contents, more work has still to be done. Inside the house, further rooms will be repaired and opened to the public in future years. In the gardens, repair of the eighteenth-century Orangery is under way. Having opened the brewhouse, smithy and carriage-houses, the Trust continues to repair the stableyard buildings. But the most important task has been achieved: Calke lives again.

The Drawing Room curtains of yellow and white silk being woven on traditional hand looms at De Vere Mills, Castle Hedingham in Essex

The Entrance Hall showing Sir John Harpur Crewe's prize cattle and the cabinet carved by Sir John Gardner Wilkinson

CHAPTER SIX

THE HOUSE: EXTERIOR AND INTERIOR

THE SOUTH FRONT

The south and principal front is a four-square Baroque design with corner pavilions, built for Sir John Harpur by an unknown architect and completed, as the lead rainwater heads indicate, in 1703. The pavilions are defined by giant fluted pilasters with Ionic capitals of unusual form (see p.24).

This is the only front to be built entirely of dressed stone, marking its importance as the entrance front. Sir John might have preferred his house to face east because the sharp rise in the ground right by the south front prevented it being seen to advantage, but orientation had been determined by the Elizabethan building.

During the 1720s Sir John paid a great deal of attention to the improvement of the approach from the south. Avenues of trees had been planted on the main axial approaches, but their visual effect was impaired by the high ground around the house. In 1721, therefore, Charles Bridgeman was paid 3 guineas 'for a Draft for the alteration of the Ground before the house'. Powder was brought to blow up the stone and in 1732 Francis Smith of Warwick was paid 'for working and laying down the Pavement in the Front of Caulk House'. Three years earlier Smith had built a flight of stone steps up to the Saloon door to designs by James Gibbs.

The last important change to the south front was the addition of a Greek Revival portico with Ionic columns added by Sir Henry Harpur in 1806–8 to the designs of William Wilkins the Elder.

THE EAST FRONT

When the building of Calke was under way, Sir John Harpur decided that the design was not entirely to his liking and the east front provides the clearest evidence of his change of mind. At first sight, it appears symmetrical, but closer examination shows it is not, because Sir John changed the design of the corner pavilions. In the eighteenth century the asymmetry was masked by a staircase leading to twin doorways in the middle of the front, but these were swept away when the balcony was built by Sir Henry Harpur in the early years of the nineteenth century to provide a view of the park from the Library. Originally this front overlooked the formal gardens.

THE WEST FRONT

Like the east front, this is not symmetrical because of the awkward planning of the pavilions. It is the only front to retain the original type of sash windows throughout. The rendering was renewed in the 1960s.

THE ENTRANCE HALL

In marked contrast to the imposing exterior of the house, the Entrance Hall is small and unassuming. The visitor is greeted by the staring heads of Sir John Harpur Crewe's prize cattle that have hung on the walls here since the middle of the nineteenth century.

It was not the original intention to put the main entrance to the house at basement level: in the eighteenth century, visitors climbed a broad flight of stone stairs on the south front, up to the Great Hall on the first floor. In 1807 the steps were replaced by the portico and this hall was created by the Derby architect Henry Isaac Stevens for Sir George Crewe in 1841.

As the hall is situated below the great void of the Saloon, the flue from the cast-iron stove was ingeniously made to travel under the floor to the nearest chimneystack.

On a stand inside the door is a collection of riding whips, accumulated over several generations, and two leather mailbags with engraved brass labels, in which letters were carried to and from the public post. There are also two table letter-boxes.

PICTURES

97 *Figures fishing in a rocky landscape*
Manner of Francesco Zuccarelli

98 *Landscape*
Manner of Jan Asselyn

FURNITURE

Six Victorian high-back chairs in Jacobean style.

A pair of late seventeenth-century settees with ebonised frames, upholstered in later crimson plush.

Four early nineteenth-century four-tier whatnots with ebonised column supports.

A seventeenth-century two-tier cupboard, painted with stars and faces of the sun and moon.

China cabinet containing a variety of oriental and English china and surmounted by a late nineteenth-century Royal Worcester figure of a pug dog. This glass-fronted cabinet was adapted by Sir John Harpur Crewe from a chimney-piece carved by the famous Egyptologist Sir John Gardner Wilkinson (1797–1875) for his house at Brynfield in Glamorganshire. Gardner Wilkinson was a cousin of Georgiana, wife of Sir John.

Nineteenth-century oak table with octagonal legs and a grey top of fossil marble.

CLOCK

Late eighteenth-century oak long-case clock with brass mounts and mahogany bandings and mouldings.

Sir John Gardner Wilkinson, the father of British Egyptology who spent many years in Egypt from 1821 studying ancient monuments and transcribing the hieroglyphic inscriptions. He was a cousin of Georgiana, Lady Harpur and left Sir John his library, sketchbooks and notes

SCULPTURE

Bust of Henry Harpur-Crewe by David Williams-Ellis, 1987.

CARICATURE ROOM

This room is a variation on the more familiar country-house print room. In place of engraved landscapes, views of buildings and other decorative subjects, there are satirical cartoons of contemporary events in high society and politics, pasted onto the walls. Many of the best-known caricaturists of the day are represented, including Rowlandson, Gillray and Cruikshank.

Most of the rooms on this storey were domestic offices, but the Caricature Room and adjoining rooms at the south-east corner of the house were used by the family as private drawing-rooms or 'parlours' because they caught the sun and were close to the garden entrance.

It is not known exactly when this room was created, but most of the prints date from the late 1790s and early 1800s, when Sir Henry Harpur was altering the house. Sir Henry's son George, later the 8th Baronet, is known to have taken an interest in caricatures and was working on the room in 1825. An undated letter, apparently written to Sir George by a schoolfriend, contains a tantalising reference: 'I shall bring no caricatures . . . how scurvily my last were used'.

When the prints were recently removed for conservation, more were found underneath, up to three deep, suggesting constant revision of the part-formal, part-haphazard arrangement. The green 'stained' lining paper and decorative flock border recreate the early nineteenth-century scheme. The printed borders were provided by the print publisher Ackerman.

FURNITURE

Late eighteenth-century kingwood and mahogany serpentine commode with ormolu mounts.

Early eighteenth-century cabinet veneered in walnut, the upper door enclosed by brass wire mesh, English.

A Regency bow front, black japanned cabinet, English, c.1810.

THE LOBBY

In the house built by Sir John Harpur in the opening years of the eighteenth century, the grand entrance was on the first floor, but there was an entrance on the ground floor for everyday use. This took the form of an arcaded passage, running east to west across the width of the house. It was later cut across by Sir George Crewe's Entrance Hall (see p.45), and the Lobby is the surviving part.

PICTURES

618 *Sir John Harpur Crewe*
Signed and dated R.H., 1877
Overpainted photograph

610 *Portrait of a young girl*
English School, later nineteenth century
Watercolour

99 *Figures on a road by a windmill*
J. Tonneau (fl.1864–91)
Signed and dated 1876

FURNITURE

Chamber organ, purchased in 1752, in a rare unaltered state. The design of the case bears a strong resemblance to work by the London cabinet-maker William Hallett.

THE PRINCIPAL STAIRS

The staircase arrangement of Sir John Harpur's house was very unusual. Originally the principal, or 'best', stairs were matched a few yards to the west by a second staircase of the same plan and dimensions, called the 'White Stairs'. These were replaced in 1842 by the present 'Stone Stairs', seen later in the tour.

The principal staircase is an example of the early eighteenth-century craftsmanship, of oak with veneers of burr yew. The plaster architraves around the windows are original but the panelled plasterwork on the walls is of later date.

The finely moulded plaster cornice at the top of the stairwell bears the Harpur crest and a monogram combining the initials of Sir John Harpur and his wife, Catherine Crewe.

Through the tall windows the inner courtyard can be glimpsed. Despite alterations, it gives some idea of the appearance of the Elizabethan house around which the present house was built.

PAINTINGS

75 *Portrait of a gentleman with a miniature spaniel*
North Italian School, c.1600

609/610 *Two children on a terrace/Two ladies on a terrace*
Fanny Corbaux (1812–83)
Watercolours

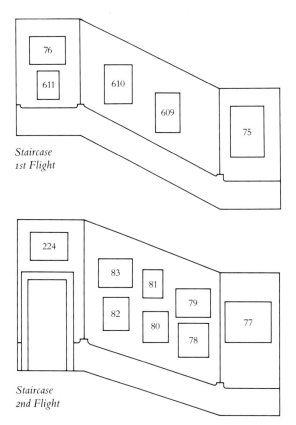

*Staircase
1st Flight*

*Staircase
2nd Flight*

Four works by Fanny Corbaux, a miniature portrait painter, are at Calke, and the subjects may well be members of the Crewe family.

76 *A saddled bay hunter in a landscape, beside a fence*
Clifton Tomson (1775–1828)
Signed and dated Nottingham 1810
The identity of the horse is not known, but is presumably one of Sir Henry Crewe's hunters, painted in the same year as No.179 in the Library.

611 An illuminated address to Richard Fynderne Harpur Crewe Esq. from the tradesmen of Melbourne and Ashby-de-la-Zouch in celebration of his twenty-first birthday in 1901.
E. Morton of Birmingham
The text is surrounded by hand-painted views of the estate.

77 *Fleacatcher*
John Nost Sartorius (1759–1828)
Signed and dated 1777
This painting forms a set with *Trentham* (No.176) and *Goldfinder* (No.174), both in the Library. The setting is almost certainly Newmarket Heath, with the Rub-

bing House on the right, the building where horses were washed down after their exertions.

79 *A woman spinning in a farmyard setting*
Manner of Francis Wheatley (1747–1801)
Wheatley developed the nostalgia then current for the simplicity of cottage life. This painting shows signs of damage, probably due to bad restoration.

78 *Saint Augustine*
Spanish School, seventeenth century

81 *A man playing a flute*
Dutch School, mid-seventeenth century

80 *Children melting wax*
Copy after Godfried Schalken (1643–1706)
Although Isabel Harpur Crewe describes this work as 'maybe Joseph] Wright of Notts and Derby', it is a copy of an engraving after a painting at Brussels by Schalken, who specialised in candle-lit scenes.

83 *A bay hunter outside a stable entrance*
Clifton Tomson (1775–1828)
Signed and dated Nottingham 1810
Painted the same year as No.76 (see above) and No.179 in the Library. Again, probably one of Sir Henry Crewe's hunters.

82 *Portrait of a young man in armour*, half length
Anglo-Dutch School, *c*.1650

224 *A spotted grey mule with two lurchers and a groom in a stable*
John Ferneley Senior (1782–1860)
Inscribed Melton Mowbray 1850

85 *Two figures with poultry*
English School, *c*.1700

612 An illuminated address to Sir John Harpur Crewe, Bt, from the inhabitants of Ticknall, Calke and Repton Priory congratulating him on his son and heir attaining his majority.
William Barn, 1867

On either side of the above are carved alabaster plaques of William Pitt and Horatio Nelson in profile. Georgiana, Lady Crewe's father, later Vice-Admiral William Lovell, took part in the Battle of Trafalgar as a midshipman on the battleship *Neptune*.

86 *The Council of Horses*
John Ferneley Senior (1782–1860)
John Ferneley, of Melton Mowbray in Leicestershire, painted hunting scenes and horse paintings of the highest quality. But *The Council of Horses*, painted for Sir John Harpur Crewe in 1850, is unique in his oeuvre. It illustrates one of John Gay's *Fables*, written in 1727, describing how a proud, young unbroken colt 'with mutiny had fir'd the train and spread dissension

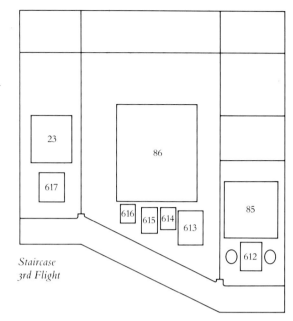

Staircase 3rd Flight

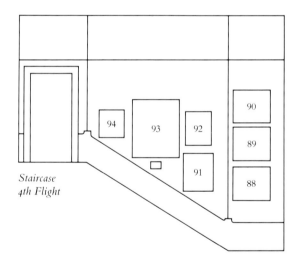

Staircase 4th Flight

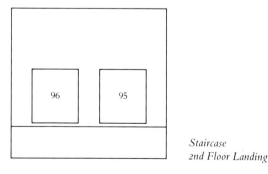

Staircase 2nd Floor Landing

through the plain' by refusing to be broken in and advising the other horses not to work for Man. This is the beautiful bay horse standing up on the left. All the horses agree until an old horse steps forward: the large dark brown horse with four white stockings and a white face. Old and wise, he rebukes the young colt:

When I had health and strength like you
The toils of servitude I knew.
Now grateful man rewards my pains
And gives me all these wide domains.
At will I crop the year's increase,
My latter life is rest and peace.

The poem ends:

The tumult ceased: the colt submitted
And like his ancestors was bitted

616 An illuminated address to Miss Crewe from the inhabitants of Ticknall, on her attaining her majority in 1898.
Miss Crewe was Hilda, eldest daughter of Sir Vauncey, who as Mrs Mosley inherited Calke on the death of her father in 1924.

615 An illuminated address to Sir John and Lady Harpur Crewe on the occasion of their son Vauncey attaining his majority in 1867, from the tenants of Smisby, Derbyshire.
Bemrose and Sons, Derby

614 A painting of the Harpur Crewe coat of arms with explanation of the quarterings, c.1812.

613 An illuminated address to Richard Fynderne Harpur Crewe from the tenants of the Derbyshire portion of the estate on the occasion of his twenty-first birthday, 5 April 1901.
E. Morton of Birmingham

23 *Ferry Carondelet and his secretary*
After Sebastiano del Piombo (c.1485–1547)
The original of this work by del Piombo is in the Thyssen Collection. Painted in Rome c.1512, it portrays the Emperor Maximilian's envoy to Pope Julius II.

617 An illuminated address to Sir John Harpur Crewe, Bt, from the tradesmen at Ashby-de-la-Zouch, on the occasion of Sir Vauncey Harpur Crewe attaining his majority, 14 October 1867.

90 *Spangle and Reveller*
John Ferneley Senior (1782–1860)
Signed, inscribed and dated 1843
Isabel Harpur Crewe described Spangle as a 'white horse . . . belonging to Sir John Harpur Crewe when he was a boy of sixteen, and a great favourite'.

89 *Queen Mab*
John Ferneley Senior (1782–1860)
Signed, inscribed and dated 1842
The mare wears a side saddle and is shown standing outside the front door of Calke.

88 *A bay hunter in a landscape*
Thomas Weaver (1774–1843)
Signed and inscribed 'Shrewsbury', dated 1819

Queen Mab, Lady Crewe's mare, standing by the front door of Calke Abbey; painted in 1842 by John Ferneley Senior (89)

Portraits of four of the children of Sir John Harpur, 4th Baronet, painted in 1718: *left*, Edward and Catherine by John Verelst (96); *right*, Henry, who succeeded his father in 1741, and John by Charles D'Agar (95)

Thomas Weaver was a Shropshire artist, noted for his animal paintings, and much patronised by Sir George Crewe.

92 *Portrait of a young man wearing a red cloak and lace cravat*
Attributed to Thomas Hawker (*c*.1641–*c*.1721)
Hawker may have been chief assistant to Lely at the time of the latter's death in 1680, and was his close but pedestrian disciple.

91 *An old man writing a book by candlelight*
By or after Godfried Schalken (1643–1706)
Like No.80, this was attributed to Joseph Wright of Derby, but is another version of a painting attributed to Schalken, sold in New York in 1989.

93 *Sir Lovell Benjamin Lovell in Hussar uniform*
T. W. Mackay (active 1826–1853)
Sir Lovell Lovell (1786–1861) was the brother of Georgiana, Lady Crewe's father, Admiral Lovell, and like him a hero of the Napoleonic Wars.

94 *Portrait of a girl in a brown dress*
Manner of Thomas Murray (1663–1735)

96 *Portrait of Edward and Catherine, younger children of Sir John Harpur, 4th Bart.*, 1718
John Verelst (fl.1689–1734)
It seems odd that Sir John commissioned two different artists to paint four of his children in two groups of two in the same year, particularly when the style of the artists is so different (see No.95 below).

95 *Portrait of Henry and John Harpur*, 1718
Charles D'Agar (1669–1723)
A pair with No.96 above, but stylistically more advanced. Henry was the eldest son, and inherited Calke in 1741.

Wemyss-ware pig sitting on the windowsill of the principal stairs

FURNITURE

Four mahogany Hepplewhite-style armchairs.
A William and Mary walnut cabinet on stand.
A Regency black japanned writing cabinet, the upper section with glazed doors, the lower with cupboards.

CERAMICS

Two early twentieth-century Wemyss-ware pigs, alluding to the boar of the Harpur crest.
A pair of turquoise majolica seats with pink flowers and yellow ribbons, c.1870.
A late nineteenth-century Minton majolica seat, made up of bamboos tied with blue ribbons.

METALWORK

An unusual pair of large enamelled metal covered jars simulating oriental porcelain, late nineteenth century.

THE SALOON

The Great Hall, known as the Saloon since the early nineteenth century, was the original entrance hall. In the eighteenth century, apart from the family portraits, it was sparsely furnished, providing a suitable place for entertaining a large number of guests. In 1748 it contained only 'two marble tables upon veneered frames, a large grate and two walnut chairs with matted bottoms'.

During the nineteenth century the room was adapted to suit the tastes of successive baronets. Although the Saloon was not included in Sir Henry's campaign of alterations, he probably filled in the arches from the stairs. He certainly made the room more comfortable by the purchase of a new carpet, curtains and window blinds, 8 pedestal lamps with double burners, 2 Grecian couches and 24 chairs to match, all bought in 1806–7 from the fashionable London firm of Marsh & Tatham. This furniture can be traced in the house inventories until the middle of the last century, but the only survivals today in the room are the pedestal lamps on yellow scagliola columns and the Grecian couches. Of the 24 chairs, only 6 are known to survive, found in 1984 in pieces in the Scullery.

In Sir George's time the Saloon was used as a chapel when the weather made it undesirable to walk to church at Ticknall or Calke. Accordingly, its contents included a large organ, a hand organ, prayer cushions, a Bible and a prayer book. Prayer benches were kept in the Butler's Pantry for use when required. Sir

The Saloon in 1886

George, author of several religious pamphlets including 'An Exhortation to diligent attendance upon the Lords Supper', 1843, conducted the services.

In 1841 the Derby architect Henry Isaac Stevens was called in to design the coffered ceiling and to straighten out the east end of the room, where he reinstated the original panelling and Corinthian pilasters and provided a new chimney-piece. The upper parts of the wall were divided into panels for the more effective display of the family portraits.

It was during Sir John Harpur Crewe's time that the Saloon acquired its present appearance. Each year the Saloon, and indeed the house as a whole, became more like a museum of natural history. The Saloon was photographed in 1886, when the room looked much as it does today, with the deer heads, antlers and the Indian buffalo skull on the north wall.

PAINTINGS

The portraits, which span the period from 1669 to 1828, are almost all of members of the Harpur family or of close relations. It is noticeable, however, that the only relations included are those which represent connections with notable families.

318 *Portrait said to be of Viscount Cullen*
English School, *c.*1710
The mother of Charles, 4th Viscount Cullen (1687–1716), Catherine Willoughby, was the sister-in-law of Sir John Harpur, 3rd Bt. As it was unusual for noblemen to be painted in their own liveries, the subject of this portrait shown holding the horse on a lunging cavesson may be a groom.

319 *Jemima, Duchess of Kent*
Charles D'Agar (1669–1723)
Jemima Crewe (d.1728) was a sister of Catherine, wife of Sir John Harpur, 4th Bt.

320 *Portrait of an unknown man*
Attributed to Thomas Murray (1663–1735)

321 *Elizabeth, Countess of Arran*
John Closterman (1660–1711)
Another sister of Catherine, wife of Sir John Harpur, 4th Bt.

322 *Unknown woman*, possibly *Lady Annabel Grey, Lady Glenorchy*
Attributed to Maria Verelst (1680–1744)

307 *Portrait of a lady called Anne Harpur*
Attributed to Isaac Whood (1689–1752)
Of the two Anne Harpurs, the first was a daughter of the 3rd Baronet: the portrait is too late to be her. The other Anne was one of the daughters of Sir John Harpur, 4th Bt, who died in infancy. It is possible that

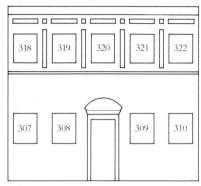

Saloon West wall

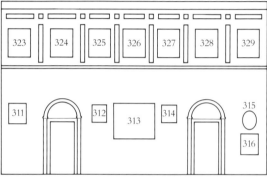

North wall

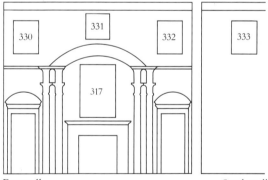

East wall   *South wall*

this is the portrait of the youngest daughter of the 4th Baronet, Mary (d.1752).

308 *Sir John Harpur, 4th Baronet*
Attributed to Charles D'Agar (1669–1723)
The builder of Calke.

309 *The Hon. Catherine Crewe, Lady Harpur with a young child*
Charles Jervas (c.1675–1739)
Catherine (d.1745), younger daughter of Thomas, 2nd Baron Crewe (No.326), married Sir John Harpur, 4th Bt in 1702. Probably the picture for which Jervas was paid £30 in 1713.

310 *Jemima Harpur*
David D'Agar (fl.1724–c.1735)
Jemima was a daughter of Sir John Harpur, 4th Bt, and Catherine Crewe. In 1718 she married Sir Thomas Palmer of Carlton Hall in Northamptonshire. Paid for in November 1724.

323 *John, 3rd Duke of Rutland*
Jonathan Richardson (1665–1745)
Caroline Manners, sister of the 3rd Duke of Rutland, seen here in the Garter Robes, was the wife of Sir Henry Harpur, 5th Bt.

324 *Brigit, wife of 3rd Duke of Rutland*
Attributed to Charles Jervas (c.1675–1739)
Brigit Sutton married John Manners (No.323) in 1717. In this portrait she holds an orange, a promise of fruitfullness in marriage.

325 *A seated lady*
Manner of Sir Godfrey Kneller, c.1690

326 *Thomas, 2nd Baron Crewe*
Charles D'Agar (1669–1723) after an unknown artist
Lord Crewe (1623–97) was very wealthy but he had no sons, so his four daughters were considerable heiresses: Catherine Harpur (Nos.309 and 315); Airmine, Mrs Cartwright; Jemima, Duchess of Kent (No.319); Elizabeth, Countess of Arran (No.321). An entry in the Calke accounts book refers to a payment to 'Mr D'Agre for a picture coppyed' in October 1704; as Catherine was a younger daughter, she may not have inherited the original portrait, and thus had to have a replica made.

327 *Catherine Harpur, Lady Gough*
John Vanderbank (1694–1739)
Catherine (d.1740), daughter of Sir John Harpur, 4th Bt, and Catherine Crewe, married a Warwickshire landowner, Sir Henry Gough Bt. The portrait was paid for in 1739.

328 *A seated lady*
Manner of Sir Godfrey Kneller

329 *James, Vice Admiral, the 3rd Earl of Berkeley* (1680–1736)
After Sir Godfrey Kneller
Lord Berkeley fought in the War of the Spanish Succession, and the short war with Spain in 1719.

311 *The Hon. Charles Greville*
After George Romney
Charles Greville (1749–1809) was the brother of Frances, wife of Sir Harry Harpur, 6th Bt. He is best known as a diarist and the favourite nephew of Sir William Hamilton, who married his discarded mistress, Emma Hart.

312 *Charles Harpur*
Attributed to Thomas Beach (1738–1806)
Charles was a younger brother of Sir Harry Harpur, 6th Bt, and appears as the smallest child in Thomas Hudson's group portrait (No.313).

313 *Portrait of the three sons of Sir Henry Harpur, 5th Baronet*
Thomas Hudson (1701–79)
Isabel Harpur Crewe commented on this portrait: 'The eldest boy [John, on the right] died at school aged twelve, and the second, Henry [centre] succeeded to the Baronetcy – the third, Charles [left] became a major in the army, and died suddenly at Twyford Hall aged 27.'

The Calke account books record a payment to Thomas Hudson for 50 guineas on December 1745, which accords with the ages of the children shown. Hudson used the famous portrait of the older children of Charles I by Van Dyck at Windsor as his model for both costume and pose of the eldest boy and mastiff.

314 *Supposed portrait of James, 1st Marquis of Montrose*
Formerly attributed to Robert Walker
This portrait is a pastiche, possibly worked up from a miniature, and is not likely to be an authentic portrait. The supposed sitter, beheaded in Edinburgh in 1650, was an ancestor of the 2nd Duke of Montrose, brother-in-law to Lady Caroline Harpur, wife of the 5th Bt.

315 *Catherine Crewe, Lady Harpur*
Charles Jervas (c.1675–1739)
Wife of Sir John Harpur, 4th Bt (for another portrait, see No.305). This portrait was presented to Sir Vauncey in 1918 by the Marquis of Crewe.

316 *Portrait of Sir John Harpur, 2nd Baronet*
English School, seventeenth century
Inscribed: J.H. DEC^r 19 1669 Aet[ati] s 53
Sir John (1616–69) was buried in Calke Church, where this portrait hung as his memorial until removed in the nineteenth century. His hand rests on a skull, symbol of death, while the winged hour glass in the background and the watch and chain in the foreground allude to the brevity of life and the speed of time passing.

330 *Sir George Crewe and his son John*
Ramsay Richard Reinagle (1775–1862)
This portrait was painted in 1828 and exhibited at the Royal Academy the following year. Isabel Harpur Crewe did not like this picture of her father, Sir George: '[it] quite fails to do him justice, or to give a true idea of his character and expression'.

331 *Sir Henry Harpur, 5th Baronet*
William Aikman (1682–1731)
Sir Henry (1708–1748) had already been painted as a boy (No.95, Staircase). Here he is a young man of twenty. The portrait was paid for in 1728.

332 *Jane, Lady Crewe*
Ramsay Richard Reinagle (1775–1862)
Jane Wittaker, daughter of Thomas Wittaker, a Norfolk parson, married Sir George Crewe in 1819. This portrait, like No.330 above of her husband, was exhibited at the Royal Academy in 1829. Again Isabel Harpur Crewe did not approve: 'a bad likeness, and wanting in the refinement which was most conspicuous in her'.

317 *Lady Frances Harpur and her son Henry*
Tilly Kettle (1735–86)
Lady Frances (d.1825), the daughter of the 1st Earl of Warwick, married Sir Harry Harpur, 6th Bt, in 1762. In this superb portrait by Tilly Kettle, painted *c*.1766, she is shown with her son Henry, destined to become the 'isolated baronet'. For another portrait of Lady Frances, see No.55 in the Drawing Room.

333 *William III*
Studio of Sir Godfrey Kneller
This is a version of Kneller's state portrait of the King.

FURNITURE

Despite Sir George Crewe's occasional use of the Saloon as a chapel, he was also responsible for the installation of the billiard table, some time before 1839. Four late seventeenth-century, ebonised high-back chairs, re-covered in the nineteenth century with needlework panels mounted on velvet.

Six glazed oak display cases made by Thomas Marriott of Ticknall, the estate joiner, in 1859. The cases on the window side of the billiard table contain, respectively, collections of shells, fossils and polished stones; on the other side, two cases of varied 'curiosities' and one of minerals.

A pair of early nineteenth-century pollard oak display cases, the glazing bars of the upper doors forming interlocking Gothic lancets, now containing a collection of fossils and minerals assembled by Sir Vauncey Harpur Crewe, about 1879.

A set of ten large cases, containing (in clockwise order from the wall to the right of the windows): cormorants, shags and gannets; rabbits and hares; a spectacular diorama of pheasants, including a number of albino specimens (above); heathland birds including grouse (below); birds of prey (above); seabirds including puffins and other auks, petrels and choughs

A glazed case in the Saloon, with a collection of curiosities from Egypt and Nubia labelled by Sir Vauncey in 1870

(below); owls (above), seabirds including ducks (below); gulls and other seabirds (above); foxes and other mammals (below).

Further cases contain a pair of golden eagles mounted on rocks, a pair of white-fronted geese, a pair of ospreys with their catch (at ground level in the centre of wall opposite windows); and a crowned crane (third tier on window wall).

A pair of rectangular oak pedestal tables with bog and burr oak inlays and enrichments, and initials 'I.H.C' for John Harpur Crewe in inlaid shields, made by Thomas Marriott of Ticknall in 1856. On one stands a glazed table-top display case containing an alligator's skull, on the other a case containing a collection of 'curiosities', including part of a human skull. On a cupboard in the corner by the window is another glazed case containing a 'collection of Egyptian curiosities, brought by me from Egypt and Nubia in 1869 & 70 – Vauncey Harpur Crewe, May 5th 1870'.

A pair of ebonised, cane-seated 'Grecian couches' supplied by Marsh & Tatham in 1806–7 with dark pink chintz covers.

A late seventeenth-century ebonised beech armchair with nineteenth-century needlework panel on the seat.

An early eighteenth-century walnut armchair with vase splat back and seat covered in nineteenth-century needlework, much restored.

A set of eight Colza oil lamps (now electrified) on yellow scagliola bases, supplied by Marsh & Tatham in 1806–7.

A burr walnut grand piano by Erard of London, introduced in 1867.

TEXTILES

Wine-coloured wool velvet curtains, probably supplied by Richard Orchard of Ashby in 1872.

CERAMICS

ON THE CHIMNEY-PIECE:

A pair of blue, cream and fawn Wheildon-style splash pottery eagles, probably late nineteenth-century Portuguese.

A pair of late nineteenth-century Chinese Dogs of Fo, one red, one yellow.

A pair of tall blue and white Kangxi beaker vases.

A pair of blue and white late Ming double-gourd bottle vases.

A black, blue and white Persian pottery baluster vase.

A pair of Minton majolica jardinières with blue and white Renaissance-style relief decoration.

CLOCK

An oak three-train mantel clock by Mappin & Webb, London, presented to Richard Harpur Crewe by the Derbyshire tenants on his coming of age, 5 April 1901.

THE LIBRARY

Created in 1805 by Sir Henry Harpur. Previous baronets had few books, but Sir Henry was a man of 'superior understanding and cultivated mind', and the contents of his library bear this out. Architecture and music are well represented. A sprinkling of legal and military books indicate that, as a landowner of the time, Sir Henry had public duties to perform in spite of his aversion to society.

The library contains many comparatively modern works, suggesting that earlier books have left the house at some stage. The surviving collection reflects the usual country-house interests: fishing and riding, travel and exploration, animal management, gardening, local and county history. The family's interest in natural history is illustrated by fine colour-plate books, particularly on birds. Sir George Crewe's personal tastes are reflected by the collection of social, religious and political literature.

The furniture was supplied by Marsh & Tatham in 1806–7, and much of it survives (see below). They also provided the rolling maps attached to the bookshelves, showing counties as well as general maps of England, Wales and Europe.

PICTURES

The paintings are exclusively equestrian, the subjects including racehorses, riding horses and hunters, carriage horses, ponies and an army charger.

174 *'Goldfinder' with a groom and other horses*
John Nost Sartorius (1759–1828)
John Nost Sartorius came from a Nuremberg family of painters, several of whom specialised in horses. Three works by him are at Calke (see Nos.77 and 176), all painted in 1777. The three horses, 'Goldfinder', 'Trentham' and 'Fleacatcher' belonged to Sir Charles Sedley of Nuthall Temple near Nottingham, and these paintings may have come to Calke after his death in 1778.

173 *A grey carriage horse in a stable*
Edwin Cooper (1785–1833)

172 *A chestnut hunter in a field*
Edwin Cooper (1785–1833)

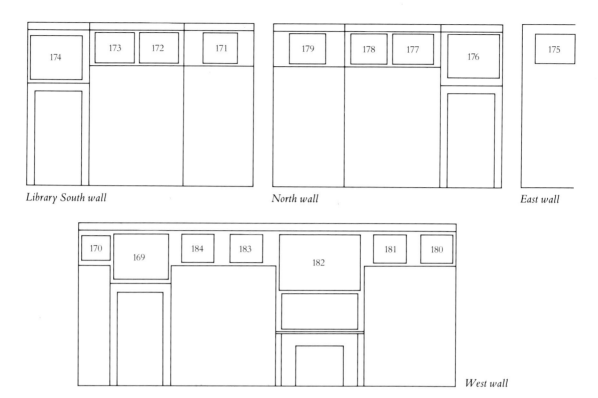

Library South wall

North wall

East wall

West wall

171 *A bay hunter in a landscape*
Edwin Cooper (1785–1833)
All three paintings are signed and dated 1827
Edwin Cooper was an East Anglian artist and therefore local to Sir George Crewe's father-in-law, the Rev. Thomas Wittaker of Harleston in Norfolk, whom Sir George used to visit.

170 *A grey pony and spaniel in a landscape*
Thomas Weaver (1774–1843)
Signed and dated Shrewsbury 1824
Thomas Weaver, born in Shropshire, was noted for animal subjects and particularly for his portraits of pedigree cattle and sheep. He painted several of the Calke prize-winning cattle. Isabel Harpur Crewe says that it is 'Mouse, a favourite pony of Sir J. Crewe, 8th Bt'.

169 *A groom with two ponies and two greyhounds in a landscape*
John Ferneley Senior (1782–1860)
Signed and dated Melton Mowbray, 1837
Isabel Harpur Crewe says that the groom is Frank Spence, Sir John Harpur Crewe's stud-groom, with two ponies that belonged to Sir John as a boy.

184 *'Furiband' with his owner, Sir Harry Harpur, and a groom*
Sawrey Gilpin (1733–1807)
Signed and dated 1774
This is one of four paintings at Calke by Sawrey Gilpin, the chief rival of George Stubbs. With Nos. 183, 181 and 180, it depicts Sir Harry Harpur's best race-horses.

183 *'Jason', a bay racehorse, with a groom in a landscape*
Sawrey Gilpin (1733–1807)
Signed and dated 1774

182 *A group of ponies in the park*
John Ferneley Senior (1782–1860)
Signed and dated Melton Mowbray 1850
This picture shows Ferneley at his most romantic: although it appears to be an imaginary ensemble, the equine subjects were all portraits, presumably of animals belonging to Sir John Harpur Crewe and painted at Calke. Isabel Harpur Crewe wrote 'Picture of horses over mantelpiece including little white pony saved from a wreck at Aldborough'.

The Library

181 *Juniper, a bay racehorse, held by a groom, probably on Doncaster racecourse; with the 1774 Doncaster Gold Cup displayed*
Sawrey Gilpin (1733–1807)
Signed and dated 1774

180 *Pilot, a grey racehorse with a jockey up, in a racecourse setting*
Sawrey Gilpin (1733–1807)
Signed and dated 1774
Pilot is the only one of this series of four of Sir Harry Harpur's best racehorses that was home bred. There had been a stud at Calke since the seventeenth century, and Sir John Harpur brought one of the first Arabian stallions into the country at the beginning of the eighteenth century: the 'Harpur Arabian' who was to become one of the ancestors of the modern thoroughbred. The Harpur horses tended to run locally rather than at Newmarket.

179 *Sheepface, a black charger, with a groom*
Clifton Tomson (1775–1828)
Signed and dated Nottingham 1810
Clifton Tomson was a Nottingham artist, whose work includes horses, dogs, cattle and also racing, hunting and some shooting scenes. *Sheepface* is held by the groom, Stainsby, outside the front door at Calke.

178 *A saddled grey hunter in a loosebox*
John Ferneley Senior (1782–1860)
Signed and dated 1854

177 *Lofty, a skewbald carriage horse, with a greyhound*
John Ferneley Senior (1782–1860)
Signed and dated Melton Mowbray 1837
Lofty was the last of the race of skewbalds at Calke according to Isabel Harpur Crewe.

176 *Trentham*
John Nost Sartorius (1759–1828)
Signed and dated 1777
See No.174.

175 *A brown saddle horse by mounting steps*
Thomas Grimshaw (fl. 1853–64)
Signed and dated 1851
Thomas Grimshaw lived in Derby. Little is known of
his work.

FURNITURE

A suite of oak furniture, banded in ebony, supplied
by the London firm of Marsh & Tatham in 1806–7,
comprising: Oak pier cupboards with black marble
tops and brass lattice doors lined with pleated red silk;
A set of library chairs with cane seats and backs, consisting of 10 chairs, 2 armchairs and 2 bergère chairs;
A chaise longue and 2 firescreens. The squab cushions
are covered in red and white chintz made by Morris &
Co., now very faded.
Oak writing table with ebonised key pattern frieze
moulding and bronze lion masks at the corners on
turned and fluted legs. This was also supplied by
Marsh & Tatham in the same year. Like the adjoining
tables, it is crowded with objects, including paper-
weights, a small carved elephant, a set of letter-scales,
a silver-mounted ostrich egg ornamented with boar's
tusks and a cast bronze figure of the Kaiser on
horseback.
Two Victorian upholstered X-frame chairs and a prie-
dieu chair covered with needlework.
A late eighteenth-century marquetry and oak Pembroke table. Octagonal walnut table with lion feet and
frieze, carved with scrolls and scallop shells, bought in
1848. Large circular table of burr and bog oak with
inlaid geometrical pattern on the top, probably made
by Thomas Marriott, the estate joiner, in the 1850s.
A mid-Victorian chaise longue with raised chair back
at the foot.
A pair of library globes, celestial and terrestrial, on
tripod stands, made by W. & A. K. Johnston of Edinburgh, c.1870.

CARPETS

Twentieth-century patterned red Axminster carpets
laid over fitted nineteenth-century machine-made
Brussels carpet. The latter may be the carpet included
in Marsh & Tatham's bill.

THE BOUDOIR

Until about 1860, the Boudoir and the two rooms
beyond it comprised one of the principal apartments
of the house, forming a private suite of rooms for an
important guest or member of the family. An apartment generally consisted of a bedroom, a closet (a
bathroom/servant's room) and another room, vari-
ously described as a dressing-room or withdrawing-
room. In the early eighteenth century this room was
known as the Inner Drawing Room to the Best Apartment; that is, a private sitting-room entered from the
principal drawing-room (now the Library) in the suite
reserved for royalty or other important guests. Sir
John Harpur himself had his apartment directly above,
on the second floor.
    In 1821 Sir George Crewe refurbished the suite as
his own apartment, and the Inner Drawing Room
became Lady Crewe's Sitting Room or Boudoir. The
room has probably changed little since that time, but
has not been in regular use for many years.

PICTURES

Sir George collected more pictures than any of his
family, and the Boudoir is furnished with a large number of his small cabinet pictures. Though not all by
the famous artists Sir George probably imagined, the
mix of family portraits, Dutch genre scenes and Italian
Renaissance pictures is typical of the period. Of particular interest are, on the fireplace wall:

Four portraits of the Harpur family
William Hoare (1706–99)
Pastels, all signed and dated 1744
Above the door is Lady Caroline, wife of Sir Henry
Harpur, 5th Bt; above the left-hand bookcase is their
only daughter, Lucy; and above the right-hand book-
case are portraits of two of their sons, John and Henry.

Richard Harpur-Crewe (1880–1921)
S. L. Brookes
Signed and dated 1922
A posthumous portrait of Sir Vauncey's only son.

Among the other paintings are, on the opposite wall:

(top left)

The Israelites gathering manna in the Wilderness
Jacob de Wet (1610–71)
De Wet was a pupil of Rembrandt and noted for his
biblical scenes.

(top, above large cabinet)

The Rest on the Flight, with angels
Giuseppe Chiari (1654–1727)
A pupil of Carlo Maratta, Chiari painted small
devotional images of this kind for collectors visiting
Rome on the Grand Tour. It was probably bought by
Sir Harry Harpur, 7th Bt.

(top, to right of gilt mirror on north wall)

Still-life with Dead Birds
Joris van der Hagan (c.1615–69)

The Annunciation
Attributed to Lorenzo di Credi (*c*.1458–1537)
On panel
Just possibly the central panel from the predella of the Pistoia altarpiece by Credi and Verrocchio.

The Holy Family
(?) Roman, mid-sixteenth century
Rather unusually painted on slate, by a follower of Raphael.

Hounds putting up a swan
Abraham Hondius (*c*.1625/30–91)
On panel
Hondius emigrated from Holland to England by 1674, where he specialised in 'beasts and hunting pieces'.

The room also contains copies of famous paintings, such as *The Children of Charles I* by Van Dyck (left of exit door), and *The Madonna della Sedia* by Raphael (above exit door), as well as of less exalted Dutch pictures.

To the right of the fireplace is a small eighteenth-century watercolour sketch of Calke Abbey painted by Miss Dewe. The photographs on the table are of Godfrey and Hilda Mosley. Hilda, the eldest daughter of Sir Vauncey Harpur Crewe, lived at Calke until her death in 1949.

CERAMICS

Besides the pictures, the principal interest in the room is the collection of ceramics. In the eighteenth-century burr walnut cabinet in the centre of the opposite wall is a collection of mainly European porcelain. This includes, on the top shelf, two characteristic Chelsea red-anchor leaf dishes, and on the shelf below, some Meissen cups and saucers, together with a variety of Crown Derby plates and Chinese export ware.

In the japanned chinoiserie cabinet on the wall opposite the fireplace is a varied collection of porcelain and pottery. The porcelain is mainly Chinese export, but there is also some interesting commemorative ware; in the left-hand case is a Bloor Derby christening mug, with the monogram 'J.H.C.' (John Harpur Crewe). Also of interest is the Derby dish with a view of Calke Abbey on a lime-green ground.

Of local interest is the collection of Ticknall pottery in the other two cabinets. Though rather coarse in character, Ticknall ware was, for a period in the seventeenth century, renowned throughout eastern England. The red-glazed earthenware produced at this time was ideal for the storage of foods such as butter and milk. A typical example is the lidded jar on the second shelf of the cabinet between the windows (to the left of the teapot).

Much of the Calke collection was excavated by Matilda Lovell, a niece of Sir George Crewe, in Ticknall in the mid-nineteenth century. Among the many pieces she found are the crude female heads (to the right of the teapot) which would perhaps have been used as knife handles or finials on lids.

Also on this shelf is an egg cup for four eggs set on a hollow ring. Possibly made for Calke Abbey, where the distance between kitchen and Breakfast Room was great, the ring would have been filled with hot water via the spout and the eggs kept warm.

The most important piece in the collection is the yellow slipware dish (*c*.1720) decorated with a stag in two tones of brown.

FURNITURE

Most of the furniture is Victorian and is typically covered. An exception is the large eighteenth-century rococo carved gilt mirror opposite the fireplace. It is in the Chinese style with two ho-ho birds. Below the mirror is a glass case containing a pair of kingfishers feeding a nest of seven fledglings.

On the fireplace is an early eighteenth-century ebonised bracket clock by Charles Gretton of London. To the left of this is a gilt bronze figure of Buddha, while on the other side is an equestrian statue of Peter the Great of Russia, which stands on a malachite base.

THE YELLOW ROOM

This room was recorded in 1741 as the Yellow Room and subsequently, in 1748, as the Best Bedchamber, reserved for the most important guest. Despite its present appearance, it is easy to understand why it should have had this use, when one remembers that it looked out on to the principal formal gardens laid out in the early eighteenth century by London and Wise. It was richly furnished and contained 'A wainscot bedsted with crimson and green silk damask furniture compleat', together with six walnut chairs and a pair of festoon curtains, all of the same material.

In Sir George Crewe's day this was his dressing-room, before becoming a spare bedroom in about 1860. Its present appearance dates from the 1960s when Charles Harpur-Crewe removed these cases of taxidermy from the Dining Room during its redecoration.

THE SCHOOLROOM

Formerly the Wrought Room (probably hung with tapestries) and then Sir George and Lady Crewe's Bedroom, this became the schoolroom in about 1860.

Unlike his father Sir John Harpur Crewe, who was educated at Rugby and Trinity College, Cambridge, Sir Vauncey, born in 1846, was educated at home, and this room was probably created for this purpose. It continued to be used as a schoolroom until the Second World War when army officers were billeted in the house. Much of the room's dilapidation dates from the time of the army's occupation and, although it was never used as a schoolroom again, many of the children's books and toys were returned to the room. When the National Trust took over the house in 1985 they found the room much as it looks today.

From the Schoolroom the route leads up a narrow staircase to Sir Vauncey's boyhood bedroom, the first in a series of rooms on the east side of the building.

SIR VAUNCEY HARPUR CREWE'S BEDROOM

This room with its Victorian wallpaper remains much as it was in Sir Vauncey's youth in the mid-nineteenth century. Above the bed and fireplace are hunting trophies, with collections of shells and fossils in a mid-nineteenth-century glazed cabinet to the left of the bed. Elsewhere the haphazard accumulation of objects, including a prodigious collection of walking-sticks of of every size and shape, is left as found by the National Trust.

THE NURSERIES, BIRD LOBBY, GARDNER WILKINSON LIBRARY AND OAK BEDROOM

The visitor passes through the semi-derelict Day and Night Nurseries before reaching the Bird Lobby, which acquired its present eccentric appearance in the later nineteenth century with Sir Vauncey's enthusiasm for collecting stuffed birds.

Next to the Bird Lobby is the Gardner Wilkinson Library. Sir Gardner Wilkinson (1797–1875) was a great nineteenth-century antiquary and archaeologist who ranks as the father of British Egyptology. He was a cousin of Georgiana, Lady Harpur Crewe and, when he died in 1875, he left his library, his sketchbooks and all his manuscript notes to Sir John Harpur Crewe to be preserved as an heirloom. The library retains its late nineteenth-century appearance.

THE DRAWING ROOM

The principal dining room of the house until 1793–4, it was refitted as a Drawing Room by Sir Henry. The fittings remain largely unchanged, but the appearance of the room has altered radically. Recently, remains of Sir Henry's original decorative scheme were found behind the mirrors: wallpaper made to resemble grey watered silk, with strikingly coloured borders in the 'Etruscan' style. The sofa and 8 armchairs were originally covered to match in ribbed and watered oyster coloured silk with a satin stripe.

Sir George Crewe may have wanted to secure more space for his growing picture collection, for in 1833 he blocked off two windows on the wall opposite the door, and opened up the centre window. The mirrors on the end wall and on the piers between the windows are likely to have been brought in at this time to match the overmantel mirror. Sir Henry's grey watered silk decoration had been superseded by several schemes before the gold and white wallpaper in the style of Pugin was hung. It is of extremely good quality, using gold leaf, and is likely to have been hung following repairs to the house in 1841–2.

The room was substantially altered for the last time in 1855–6 by Georgiana, wife of Sir John Harpur Crewe. New yellow and white silk curtains were supplied by Jackson & Graham of Oxford Street, London, who also upholstered the chairs to match, provided an 8-foot ottoman to the left of the fireplace and made up a 'superfine crimson velvet pile carpet' to plan. All the gilding in the room was renewed and the ceiling rewashed. Lady Harpur Crewe was at first anxious about the effect, but she eventually decided that the hangings were handsome, though expressing dissatisfaction with the carpet: 'It is too *pink* to please me', she wrote, 'but candlelight may make a difference.' Her hopes were perhaps unfulfilled, because by the time the Drawing Room was photographed in 1886 the carpet had been replaced.

The method of hanging the pictures with a long wire hung over a single hook probably dates back to the middle of the nineteenth century.

PICTURES

Many portraits hang in this room, mingled with Old Masters: they depict members of the Harpur Crewe family and their Greville connections through Sir Harry Harpur's marriage in 1762 to Lady Frances Greville, daughter of the 1st Earl of Warwick.

The Drawing Room

47 *Georgiana, Lady Brooke*
Copy after George Romney
Georgiana Peachy married George, Lord Brooke, later 2nd Earl of Warwick, in 1771.

51 *Henrietta, Countess of Warwick*
Copy after Thomas Gainsborough
After the early death of his first wife, Georgiana (No.47), George Greville married Henrietta Vernon.

48 *Cattle and sheep watering*
(?) Van der Does
This archetypal Dutch landscape may be by Jacob Van der Does (1623–73) or by his son Simon (1653–*c*.1720).

49 *Sir Harry Harpur, 6th Bt*
Sir Thomas Lawrence (1769–1830)
Pastel. Inscribed and dated 1784
Together with the portrait of Sir Harry's son, Henry (No.50), this was executed by Thomas Lawrence at the age of fifteen, at his father's hotel in Devizes.

50 *Sir Henry Harpur, 7th Bt*
Sir Thomas Lawrence (1769–1830)
Pastel. Inscribed and dated 1784
See No.49 above.

602 *Henry Robert Harpur Crewe*
Octavius Oakley (1800–67)
Pencil and watercolour
Second son of Sir Henry Harpur, 7th Bt, he became Rector of Breadsall in Derbyshire.

52 *The Holy Family*
Circle of Joos van Cleve (*c*.1464–1540)

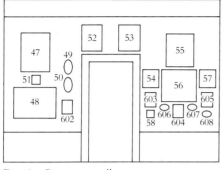

Drawing Room west wall

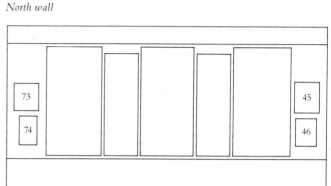

North wall

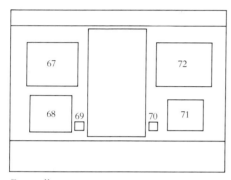

East wall

South wall

53 *Head of the Virgin*
After (?) Pompeo Batoni (1708–87)

55 *Lady Frances Harpur*
Angelica Kauffmann (1741–1807)
Inscribed on the back: *Angelica Pinx/1767*
Lady Frances Greville, daughter of Charles, 1st Earl of
Warwick, married Sir Harry Harpur in 1762.

54 *The Penitent Magdalen in the Wilderness*
Circle of Denys Calvaert (1540–1619)
On copper

603 *Sir George Crewe, 8th Bt*
Octavius Oakley (1800–67)
Pencil and watercolour

58 *Nanette, Lady Harpur*
Artist unknown
Oval miniature on ceramic of Nanette Hawkins, the
lady's maid who became mistress of Sir Henry Harpur,
the 'isolated baronet', and then in 1792 his wife.

56 *Travellers in a mountain landscape*
George Arnald (1763–1840)
Signed and dated 1804

606 *A coastline with ships*
Sir John Harpur Crewe, 9th Bt (1824–86)
Pencil and watercolour

604 *Sir John Harpur Crewe as a child*
Octavius Oakley (1800–67)
Pencil and watercolour

607 *A coastline with ships*
Sir John Harpur Crewe (1824–86)
Pencil and watercolour

57 *Abraham and Sarah*
Eighteenth-century imitator of Rembrandt

605 *Jane, Lady Crewe*
Octavius Oakley (1800–67)
Pencil and watercolour
Jane Wittaker, the daughter of a Norfolk parson,
Thomas Wittaker, married Sir George Crewe in 1819.
This picture probably dates from that time.

608 *A group of cupids* (after an Antique cameo)
Sir Thomas Lawrence (1769–1830)
Pencil and watercolour

60 *A winter landscape at sunset with figures on a frozen river*
William James Müller (1812–45)
Signed and dated 1841

59 *Figures and Horses by a Tavern*
Imitation of Barent Gael

20 *Greyhounds resting*
Sir Edwin Landseer (1802–73)

61 *An old man conversing with a seated mother and child in a river landscape*
Dutch School, early nineteenth century

Adoration of the Magi
J. Vermardel (dates unknown)
Signed
This painting, possibly after a print by Romanelli, is painted on the top of a folding table – a form of display found in Dutch houses in the eighteenth century.

66 *Boathouse in Calke Park*
John Glover Junior (fl.1808–29)

62 *Gentleman with tricorn hat*
Style of Francis Hayman (1708–66)
A letter of 1901 from Isabel Harpur Crewe to her great-aunt suggests that this is a portrait of Sir Harry Harpur, 6th Bt.

63 *A carrier's cart with a diligence approaching*
Charles Cooper Henderson (1803–77)

64 *Coaches on a Spanish road*
Charles Cooper Henderson (1803–77)

65 *A coach scene on a mountain road*
Charles Cooper Henderson (1803–77)
All three monogrammed

67 *Cattle and Deer in Calke Park*
Ramsay Richard Reinagle (1775–1862)
Exhibited at the RA in 1829.

68 *St Benedict and St Scholastica and companions in a landscape*
Attributed to Jean-Baptiste de Champaigne (1631–81)
St Benedict and his sister, St Scholastica, both died *c*.AD550. Benedict, a hermit who founded the Benedictine order, made annual visits to his sister, the first Benedictine nun, near Monte Cassino in Italy.

69 *Elizabeth Hamilton, Dowager Countess of Warwick*
English School, late eighteenth century
Oil on porcelain
Elizabeth Hamilton was Lady Frances Harpur's mother and wife of Charles, 1st Earl of Warwick. According to an inscription on the frame of the miniature, it was painted from life in about 1795 when the Countess was 75.

70 *Charles Gerard, 1st Earl of Macclesfield*
Anglo-Dutch School, *c*.1650
Miniature of Lord Macclesfield (?1620–94), a Royalist commander during the Civil War.

72 *A view of Calke Park with figures, cattle and sheep*
John Glover Junior (fl.1808–29)

71 *Soldiers playing cards in a guardroom*
Imitator of David Teniers the Younger

73 *Madonna and Child*
After Parmigianino (*c*.1503–40)
An eighteenth-century copy of a painting in the Naples Museum.

74 *(?) The Hon. Robert Greville*
Manner of L. F. Abbott (*c*.1760–1802)
Robert Greville (1751–1824) was the third son of the 1st Earl of Warwick, and Lady Frances Harpur's brother.

45 *Adoration of the Shepherds*
(?) Italian School, late seventeenth-century

46 *Cavaliers at an encampment*
Dutch School, nineteenth-century

FURNITURE

Set of 8 giltwood armchairs and sofa in the neo-classical taste, English, *c*.1794. Re-covered in yellow and white silk tissue in 1855–6. Probably those supplied by a Mr Elliott.
Upholstered ottoman supplied by Jackson & Graham of Oxford Street, London, in 1855–6, covered in the same silk as above.
Three giltwood prie-dieux chairs and 2 easy chairs without arms, mid-nineteenth century, upholstered in contemporary needlework.
A Victorian rectangular giltwood firescreen with a glazed needlework panel.
A pair of early nineteenth-century giltwood footstools on splayed feet upholstered in contemporary needlework.
A pair of early Victorian gilt two-tier semi-circular pier tables with white marble slabs on fluted legs.
A late Victorian black papier maché table with a chess-board top incorporating mother of pearl.
A pair of semi-circular satinwood pier tables in late eighteenth-century style, with tulipwood and box inlaid decoration. They support glass domes containing a carved-wood group of deer on rocks (left) and a diorama of 7 stuffed mice (right), and two smaller domes containing a shrew and a mouse.
A serpentine fronted satinwood commode in late eighteenth-century style, with white marble top, Wedgwood blue and white jasperware plaque inset

into the frieze and painted panels and decoration. On it stands a glass dome over a *tableau* of exotic birds flanked by a pair of smaller domes over Meissen-style groups of dancers.

Two similar oval oak tables on scroll legs carved with oak leaves, made by Thomas Marriott of Ticknall in 1856. On each a glazed display case containing a collection of polished stones.

An early nineteenth-century rosewood sofa table.

A nineteenth-century circular table of bird's-eye maple on hexagonal tapered stem and triangular base, on it a collection of Parian-ware figures (see below).

A rectangular table veneered in bird's-eye maple on two hexagonal tapered column legs and cross bars. The top is crowded with objects, including a pair of Burmese ebony elephants and two Eiffel Tower thermometers.

A mid-nineteenth-century black and gold table, the top in the form of an elongated octagon with spiral column supports on a quadruped base. The top has a fitted patchwork cover with black and gold valance, normally covered, like the table beyond, with a fitted blue plush cover. On the table, among a varied collection of ceramics, a large silver mounted ramshorn snuff mull, engraved with the family arms, *c.*1850.

Tall rectangular glass case containing an ivory pagoda, said to have been given to Jane, Lady Crewe, by a friend in the East India Company.

A pair of early nineteenth-century gilt wood and metal three-branch wall sconces, surmounted by eagles and suspended from masks on carved gilt ribbons.

TEXTILES

Kashmir carpet, with black and red *boteks* on a faded frieze, originally pale blue, introduced between 1856, and 1886, with matching hearthrug.

Curtains and pelmets in 'Poppy' fabric by Norris & Co, formerly of Spitalfields, supplied in 1856. The silk was an extremely expensive tissue, in which greater effects of figuring can be obtained than in the more familiar damask. By 1983 the curtains had been rotted by light damage to the point where they were turning to powder, so they were rewoven on traditional hand looms at De Vere Mills, Castle Hedingham, Essex (see p.43).

CERAMICS

A large collection of oriental blue and white porcelain, English and continental wares.

On the table in front of the centre of the end wall is a group of Copeland and Minton Parian-ware figures: a Minton figure of a trapper, flanked by a pair of

Nineteenth-century ormolu and white marble clock under a glass dome in the Drawing Room

smaller Copeland figures of a girl feedding birds and a boy with a bird's nest. There is also a group of two sleeping children, and a Crown Derby 'Stevenson and Hancock' biscuit group of Cupid asleep, watched by two nymphs.

On the chimney-piece is a set of Derby pear-shaped bottles and covered bowls by Stevenson and Hancock.

METALWORK

Early nineteenth-century gilt Colza lamp (converted to electricity) with amphora-shaped cistern and etched tulip-shaped glass shades.

Next to the fireplace, one of several black and gold Pontypool enamelled coal scuttles to be found in the house.

CLOCK

Mid-nineteenth-century ormolu and white marble mantel clock under glass dome made by E. & E. Emanuel of Portsea.

THE BREAKFAST ROOM

This room was refitted by Sir Henry Crewe in 1810 as a music room. The joinery, particularly the bold door and window architraves, is characteristic of the period. The black and gilt fillet is of the same date. The fireplace, installed in 1811, is of Derbyshire fossil limestone which resembles marble when polished, and is popularly known as Hopton marble. In practice the room has almost always been a private 'dining parlour', latterly used for afternoon tea. The only piece of furniture that illustrates the room's original use is Sir Henry's music cabinet (see below).

PICTURES

302 *The Betrayal of Christ*
After Sir Antony Van Dyck (1599–1641)
A copy of a sketch by Van Dyck for his painting in the Prado.

191 *Lucy, Duchess of Montrose, in Van Dyck dress*
Copy after Thomas Hudson (1701–79)
Lady Lucy Manners, youngest daughter of the 2nd Duke of Rutland, was a sister of Lady Caroline Harpur. She married William Graham, 2nd Duke of Montrose in 1742.

303 *A young girl watering poultry*
Attributed to Giovanni Agostino Cassana (1658–1720)

304 *An old man in armour*
(?) John Vanderbank (1694–1739) in imitation of Titian
Isabel Harpur Crewe thought this was Sir Henry Harpur, 1st Bt (d.1638), while others believed it to be Sir John Harpur of Swarkestone. In fact, it is likely to be a mid-eighteenth-century painting: there was a fashion at the time to produce fancy pictures of bogus ancestors inspired by old masters.

305c *A view of the Bay of Naples from S Martino with Vesuvius beyond and the Palazzo di Capo di Monte to the left*
Gabriele Ricciardelli (fl.1745–85)
Signed and dated 1747

305a *A view of the Bay of Pozzuoli with Baia and Ischia beyond*
Gabriele Ricciardelli
Signed

305b *A view of Naples from the east, with the Maschio Angioino, and the monastery of S Martino beyond*
Gabriele Ricciardelli
Signed and dated 1747

305d *A view of Naples seen from the west with the monastery of S Martino on the hill to the left*
Gabriele Ricciardelli
This set of four paintings is one of the treasures of Calke. Little is known of Ricciardelli, but he was able to take advantage of the vogue for Neapolitan views amongst those who had made the Grand Tour. The Harpurs, however, do not seem to have acquired these directly. Isabel Harpur Crewe states they were 'bought, I believe, by Sir Henry Crewe out of an inn at Leicester'. The English form of his Christian name in his signatures suggests that Ricciardelli was in England when these pictures were painted.

193 *(?) The poet John Gay*
Attributed to George Knapton (1698–1778)
John Gay was the author of *The Beggars Opera* and of *Fables*, written in 1727, one of which forms the

A view of Naples from the east by Gabriele Ricciardelli (305b)

inspiration for John Ferneley's painting of *The Council of Horses* (No.86, The Principal Stairs).

192 *A farmstead in winter*
Nineteenth-century English School

306 *The Card Players*
After Thedor Rombouts (1579–1637)

185 *Gentleman wearing a gold cloak*
Sir Peter Lely (1618–80)
On the back is inscribed: 'This Portrait of himself by Sir Peter Lely was presented by him to the Earl of Ferrers in gratitude to the Earl as his Patron, and was purchased by me at the unfortunate dismantling of the House at Staunton Harold by the Folly of some and the rapiery of others in June 1834. Geo. Crewe, Calke Abbey.' Although there is no doubt that Lely painted this portrait, it bears no resemblance to him.

194 *A barn interior with cattle and peasants*
Govert Dircksz Camphuysen (*c*.1624–72)

196a *Cavaliers before a walled town*
Franco-Flemish School, eighteenth-century
Pendant to No.196b below.
The uniforms suggest that these two pictures may have been painted in England.

195 *Still life of birds and flowers in a park*
Jan Weenix (1640–1719)
Signed

186 *Changing horses, the Exeter to London mail; the man leading the horse said to be Sir Henry Paton Bt*
William Davis (op.1803–49)
Signed with monogram and dated 1821

187 *Kingsey Village near Thame, Oxon*
John Linnell (1792–1882)
Dated 1826

198 *A vanitas still life*
Attributed to Edward Collier (fl.1673–1706)
The latter part of the inscription, 'thus we consume and so our lyght goes out. The time was, the time is, the time shall be', was employed by the Jacobites.

196b *Cavaliers before a walled town*
Franco-Flemish School, eighteenth-century
Pendant to No.196a above

197 *A barn interior*
Cornelis Saftleven (1607/8–81)
Signed

301 *A cavalry skirmish*
Palamedes Palamedesz, called Stevaerts (1607–38)
Signed with initials

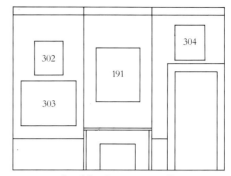

Breakfast Room west wall

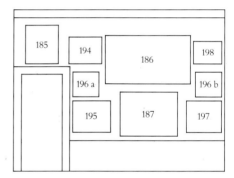

North wall

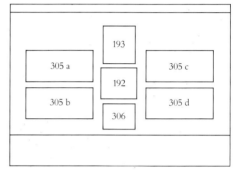

East wall

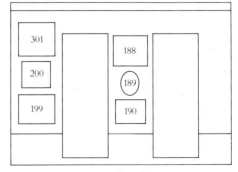

South wall

200 *Herdsmen and cattle in a river landscape*
After Aelbert Cuyp
An English copy; the original is in the Corcoran Gallery in Washington DC.

199 *The tax collectors*
Imitator of Joos van Craesbeek (*c.*1605–62)
Indistinctly initialed CB

188 *Fisherfolk on the seashore*
Manner of George Morland

189 *Lady Caroline Harpur*
English School *c.*1740
Pastel
Daughter of 2nd Duke of Rutland, she married Sir Harry Harpur, 5th Bt in 1734.

190 *Calke Hall*
The Rev. H. Palmer
Gouache
The inscription on the back reads: 'Calke Hall in Derbyshire, the seat of Sir Henry Harpur, Bt, Painted by the Rev. H. Palmer from the original in the possession of Sir John H^Y. Palmer Bt, 1823.'

Jemima, daughter of Sir John Harpur, 4th Bt, had married Sir Thomas Palmer of Carlton, Northamptonshire, in 1735. The picture shows the south front with the steps built in 1728–9. The arms on the coach are those of the 5th Bt, who died in 1748. The original painting is now in the Yale Center for British Art, New Haven, Conn.

PHOTOGRAPHS

One of the smaller photographs on the cabinet to the left of the fireplace is of Sir Vauncey in old age, carrying a gun on his shoulder.
On the easel in the corner to the left of the windows is a vignetted photograph of Richard Harpur Crewe at the wheel of his car.

FURNITURE

Overmantel glass with three bevelled Vauxhall plates, early nineteenth century.
Three giltwood armchairs, English, *c.*1794, upholstered in faded chintz. Part of the Drawing Room suite (see p.63).
A set of five mahogany early nineteenth-century dining chairs with X-frame backs, the seats upholstered in red oiled cloth.
An eighteenth-century mahogany library arm chair upholstered in yellow cotton damask.
Early nineteenth-century upholstered beechwood chaise longue in faded chintz loose cover.
Circular oak table on triangular pillar and three-cornered base, the top inlaid with alternating light and

Photograph of Richard Harpur Crewe, Sir Vauncey's son and heir, who died in 1921

dark stained oak in radiating bands, with centre roundels of pollard oak, English, *c.*1840.
Mahogany music cabinet with bronze gadrooned edge to the top and claw feet, made for Sir Henry Crewe in 1810. The shelves, originally intended for sheet music, now contain a collection of shells and minerals. On the right-hand side at the back, a tall, narrow door gives access to compartments for barrel-organ barrels. Among the objects standing on it is a glass-fronted case containing a specimen of 'fool's gold'.
(Between the windows) A late eighteenth-century mahogany cabinet, now containing a collection of minerals and shells.
A late eighteenth-century oval satinwood Pembroke table, with kingwood cross-banding and square tapering legs. The objects on top include two leather-covered letter clips and a miniature cardboard 'bookcase' of stationery items.
An early nineteenth-century dark-stained mahogany reading table with rising top.

TEXTILES

Bordered nineteenth-century Axminster carpet to an antique Hamadan design in buff, red, black and grey. Soumac hearth rug with design in pink, orange and black on blue field.

CERAMICS

A pair of turquoise cache-pots by Viellard & Co., and single, larger one of Minton turquoise majolica.
A pair of nineteenth-century Bohemian ruby baluster vases with painted panels.

THE DINING ROOM

Until the end of the eighteenth century, the first floor of the south-west pavilion was divided to form an apartment consisting of the 'Gilt Leather Room' with an adjoining lobby and two closets. In 1793 Sir Henry Harpur brought in William Wilkins the Elder to help him in his reorganisation of the interior of Calke, including the creation of a new dining-room out of the existing 4 smaller rooms. The work was finished in 1794–5. The 'man that polished the pillars in the dining room' was given 10s 6d by Sir Henry's order in February 1794, and the balance of Wilkins' account for the dining-room was paid in December of the following year. Unfortunately nothing is known about the craftsmen who worked on the room, or about the painter responsible for the inset paintings. These are after the antique in the style of Felice Giani and may possibly be the work of Vincenzo Valdrè (c.1742–1844), who painted the music room at Stowe in about 1781.

FURNITURE

Mahogany dining-table, probably bought by Sir George Crewe in 1827.

Twenty-six early nineteenth-century mahogany dining-chairs in three sets, probably supplied by the Mr Elliott who may have provided the Drawing Room chairs.

Early nineteenth-century mahogany break-front sideboard with brass curtain rails.

A pair of late eighteenth-century mahogany knife-boxes.

A late eighteenth-century fall-front bureau cabinet in 'oyster' veneer of kingwood.

The Dining Room

A seventeenth-century Italian ebony and red tortoise-shell cabinet with embossed silver mounts on a later gilt wood stand. Bequeathed by Mary Adeline, (daughter of Sir George Crewe), who died in 1930.
Two eighteenth-century circular three-tier dumb-waiters.
Two early nineteenth-century teapoys, one of Coromandel wood with undulating fluted sides, the other rectangular, of burr elm, on a tapering hexagonal stem.
A pair of ebonised child's high chairs, rails painted with gilt Chinoiserie figures, pagodas and the Harpur crest.
A pair of late nineteenth-century English glazed, japanned display cabinets.

CARPET

Machine-woven Kashan carpet with dark red ground, laid over a red, blue and orange Turkey carpet.

CERAMICS

On the chimney-piece a pair of pale blue Wedgwood jasperware pot-pourri vases, and three Paris double-handled vases.
A pair of Minton vases painted with flowers on a pink ground.
In the display cabinet by the window wall, a German figure of a pagod, with nodding head, tongue and hands.

METALWORK

Nineteenth-century bronzed brass hanging Colza lamp (now electrified).
Two Pontypool enamelled tin coal scuttles.

THE BUTLER'S PANTRY

This is the only room on the tour that has a modern appearance: the fluorescent lighting, the decoration and the sink unit all date from the 1960s when it was used occasionally as a kitchen. Originally it was a serving room, the cupboards on the south wall opposite the fireplace probably contemporary with the creation of the room in 1794. The dresser on the west wall under the windows was made in 1866.

The family meals had to make a long journey from the kitchen on the floor below to the dining-table; first, in a metal cupboard on wheels down the cold passage from the kitchen; then up to the Butler's Pantry in the lift by the fireplace; finally to be served onto plates from the warmer by the lift, heated by hot-water pipes from the adjacent range.

Outside the butler's pantry, by the Stone Stairs, is a set of servants' bells connected to pulls in the family rooms by a system of cranks and wires in 1809.

THE STONE STAIRS AND THE WEST PASSAGE

The White Stairs of Sir John Harpur's house (see p.47) were replaced in 1841 by the present Stone Stairs to improve circulation around the house. Passages were created to link the staircase landings to the west passage on all three storeys.

THE WEST PASSAGE

The west passage marks the beginning of the servants' domain. It is one of the least altered parts of the house, and retains its original, early eighteenth-century two-panelled doors. The yellow and white limewashing on the walls, combined with the drab painting of the joinery, is a rare survival of the commonplace decoration to be found in the nineteenth century in most humble cottages and the domestic quarters of country houses: it has probably not been touched at Calke since before 1924. Similar decorative schemes survive in the north passage of the first floor and in the kitchen and adjacent rooms.

THE CALKE STATE BED

A new door leads into a room that was formerly the Housemaids' Bedroom, now used to display the spectacular Calke State Bed.

Lady Caroline Manners, daughter of the 2nd Duke of Rutland, had served as a maid of honour at the marriage of Princess Anne, daughter of George II and Queen Caroline, to the Prince of Orange in March 1734. In September of the same year, she herself was married to Sir Henry Harpur, the 5th Bt. It is likely, therefore, that the bed was a gift from the Princess to mark the wedding of her maid of honour.

It is a magnificent example of Baroque upholstery, probably made for George I in about 1715. The brilliant colours of the Chinese silk hangings have hardly been exposed to light and dust, hence the need to protect the bed behind glass. The dark blue material is light in weight, like taffeta, and densely embroidered with flowers and birds. The white textile, on the other hand, is much heavier with a satin finish, boldly decorated with processions of figures, warriors on horseback, mandarins and ladies in brightly coloured robes,

The State Bed which probably came to Calke in 1734 with the marriage of Lady Caroline Manners and Sir Henry Harpur, 5th Baronet. As it was never put up, the colours of the Chinese silk hangings are astonishingly brilliant

Detail of the Chinese silk hangings of the State Bed

as well as dragons, birds, gazelles and other animals. It had been thought that gold thread was not introduced into this kind of work until later, but early eighteenth-century examples have been documented in Sweden. A particularly fascinating detail is the use of peacock feathers, tightly rolled, for the knots of the tree trunks and the markings of the butterfly wings.

The bed was never put up in the house, probably because none of the rooms in the family's part, except the Saloon, had a high enough ceiling. Notes attached to some of the pieces suggest that they may have been lent to the 1870 Midlands Counties Exhibition in Derby by Sir John Harpur Crewe. Otherwise the bed seems to have remained packed up in the next door room, where the box that contained part of it until 1985 can still be seen.

THE MUSEUM ROOM

This was originally the Housekeeper's Bedroom, her status in the hierarchy of servants reflected in the panelling. The room now contains a changing display of items found in different parts of the house and stables in 1984.

THE LAMP ROOM

The survival of this, with its lamps left ready for use the next day, is a reminder that electricity was not introduced to Calke until 1962, and even then only to the principal rooms. When the Duchess of Devonshire launched the Calke Abbey appeal in 1985, she recalled seeing the house for the first time over twenty years before, on a wet and dark November evening, glowing with the light from hundreds of candles.

THE LAUNDRY STAIRS

The staircase down to the kitchen passes by the Laundry, built in 1812 and not at present shown to visitors. The Laundry Stairs were built to the designs of the architect Henry Marley Burton as part of works carried out in 1865–7 to improve circulation and to modernise the domestic arrangements.

THE KITCHEN

This lofty room is shown as it was found by the Trust. It was fitted up as a kitchen by Sir Henry Harpur in 1794 when the previous kitchen was converted into the Housekeeper's Room and Butler's Pantry (see p.69). The kitchen clock by Whitehurst of Derby dates from that year, and some of the original shelves and worktops supplied for £62 19s 6d in 1795 can still be identified. The space now occupied by the kitchen

The Cook's Closet with eighteenth-century wooden fittings. Blue was often chosen for use in kitchens and associated areas because it was believed that the colour repelled flies

does not feature in the Calke inventories of the 1740s, but may possibly have been intended to serve as a chapel. The painted keystone of the huge fireplace repeats the old adage 'Waste Not Want Not'. The kitchen has not been used since the 1920s after the dramatic reduction in staff that occurred in most country houses after the First World War. Sir Vauncey normally employed about 27 servants at Calke but after his death in 1924 the figure was reduced to six. The Kitchen gradually fell out of use in favour of the smaller and more conveniently sited Still Room in the south-west pavilion, with Sir Vauncey's panelled study next door converted into a dining room. In 1928 the old kitchen was finally abandoned.

The wide fireplace was originally a roasting hearth, before which the meat was cooked on spits and racks. By the 1840s the cast-iron oven had been introduced. The present Beeston Boiler for hot water was installed by Colonel and Mrs Mosley in the 1920s when the kitchen had fallen out of use and the roasting hearth was redundant. Above the roasting range is a jack, operated by a fan in the flue turned by the force of the draught. The fan axle was then geared through the wall to rotate the three long spit hooks suspended from the horizontal bar. The closed cast-iron range in the secondary fireplace was supplied by R. Russell & Sons of Derby in 1889. Along the north wall there is a mid-nineteenth-century stove of cast iron and brickwork,

used for stewing, making sauces and as a hotplate for soup boilers, fish kettles, etc.

The Scullery on the north side of the kitchen occupies part of an earlier attached building that formerly housed the bakehouse, brewhouse and wash house. It was designed for the wettest and dirtiest kitchen tasks. The sinks and draining-boards were used for washing up and for the preparation of vegetables: peelings and stalks would be emptied into the lead-lined chute in the northern wall, discharging into a cast-iron vessel in the passage beyond, where it was turned into mash for the pigs.

The Cook's Closet on the south side of the kitchen served as a pantry and workroom, replacing the 'pastry' associated with the earlier kitchen. The range of cupboards and drawers held the cook's preserves and stores of cereals, together with her cake and pie tins, moulds and other working equipment. A seventeenth-century oak spice cupboard, probably re-covered from the earlier kitchen, was recased and mounted on the east wall. The little staircase leads up to the Cook's Bedroom (not on view).

The visitor leaves the house through the west door, passing on the way the open doors of two store rooms shown as they were found, and takes the path back up the hill to the stables. The tour of the stables and other buildings is described on page 76.

The painted keystone over the fireplace in the kitchen. The walls are decorated in characteristic nineteenth-century yellow limewashing, probably last redecorated before 1900

CHAPTER SEVEN

THE PARK AND GARDENS

THE PARK

Until opened to the public for the first time in October 1985, Calke Park was a secret world. The lodges at Ticknall and Heathend hinted tantalisingly at the hundreds of acres of fine English landscape beyond them, seen only by a privileged few.

The privacy of the park is due partly to its seclusion from public roads, partly to the reclusive nature of the Harpurs who bought and landscaped as much land as possible within view of their house. The park is centred on a wooded valley containing a stream, now dammed to form a chain of ponds, flowing eastwards into a larger valley flooded today by the Staunton Harold reservoir. The park landscape is rich and varied, from gnarled oaks and bracken to rolling, close-cropped grassland punctuated by groups of strategically placed specimen trees.

The timeless areas of old oaks and bracken at the core of the park represent the last remnants of a large tract of medieval woodland lying south of the River Trent, and the original seventeenth-century park of 185 acres or less was formed by the grouping together of three medieval woodlands: Castle Close and Roche and Bowley Woods. Roche Wood, south of Betty's Pond, derived its name from the French word for rocky or stony; disused quarries can still be seen there, and this part of Calke parish was evidently more than the medieval plough could cope with. Castle Close commemorates the former existence of a mysterious building known as Cheriston Castle, which finally disappeared in the seventeenth century. Castle Close and Bowley Wood, which in the sixteenth century fell outside the bounds of Calke parish, were purchased by Robert Bainbridge (d.1613) or his son. In all justice the Bainbridges should be regarded as the founders of Calke Park: in the late sixteenth and early seventeenth centuries woodlands all round Calke were being felled, and the Bainbridges may well have bought and preserved these undeveloped tracts adjoining Calke as a conscious reaction against woodland clearance. The first mention of a park at Calke does not occur until 1640 when the Harpurs had come into possession, so it is unclear whether the Bainbridges enclosed their newly purchased woodlands as a park. The park is not represented on Speed's map of Derbyshire, made in 1610.

In the seventeenth century Calke Park was first and foremost a deer reserve, and evidence of planned landscape features begins only in 1712, when avenues of trees were planted across the park to align with the axes of Sir John Harpur's new house. At Calke, as at many other places, the avenues extended beyond the limits of the park into tenanted farmland, to create an illusion of spaciousness.

The earliest plan of Calke, dateable to 1761, shows the formal landscape at Calke towards the end of its life. In the previous year, Sir Harry, the 6th Baronet, had come of age, and almost immediately he began to enlarge and remodel the park. William Emes was employed in 1764–5 to make 'Plans and Estimates for Gardens & Pleasure Ground at Calke', which unfortunately do not survive, but the present walled gardens were not built until 1773 and Sir Harry seems to have acted as his own landscape gardener. In 1769 he extended the park to the south. The newly added land, in contrast to the rugged character of the original park, consisted mainly of old ridge and furrow ploughland of medieval or late Tudor date, mostly converted to pasture by the mid-seventeenth century. A flock of Portland sheep was introduced here to graze. Portland sheep, a rare breed, have been kept at Calke ever since, and it is believed that they would have become extinct if the Harpurs had not preserved them. A few years later a new deer shelter, now ruinous, was built in the new addition amongst a clump of trees, to

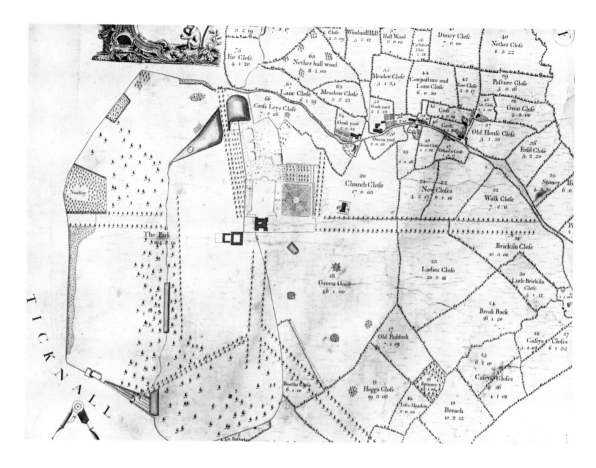

The 1761 plan of Calke Park showing the formal gardens
and landscape schemes created by Sir John Harpur at the
beginning of the eighteenth century

encourage the herds of red and fallow deer to ven-
ture from their more natural habitat elsewhere in
the park. It was apparently in the 1770s that High-
land cattle were introduced to Calke, and the
nineteenth-century accounts refer frequently to
renewals of the stock, brought directly by rail from
Scotland. Unfortunately these cattle are not to be
seen at Calke today as they were dispersed in 1886
according to the will of Sir John Harpur Crewe.

During the 1770s Sir Harry felled most of the
avenues of trees just when they were probably
beginning to look mature and well established.
Near the house only a few were suffered to remain,
including a group of limes by the west end of the

church, but substantial remains of the avenues can
be found in the more remote and wooded areas of
the park. In 1779, the park was extended to the east,
engulfing part of the village street of Calke, whose
farming population was rapidly diminishing. Ten
years later, about 167 acres of land were added at
the north-east corner of the park, mainly from the
parish of Melbourne which was then being
enclosed. In 1805, the land now occupied by the
lime avenue between Middle Lodge and Ticknall
Lodge was added to provide a more graceful
approach to the park.

These two lodges, together with a third at the
Heathend entrance, were designed by William
Wilkins the Elder and finished in 1807. The Ticknall
lime avenue was planted in 1846 to commemorate
the birth of Sir Vauncey Harpur Crewe; there were
originally 82 trees in all, purchased from an Ashby
nurseryman for a shilling each.

(*Above*) Longhorn cattle with their minders, in Calke Park in the 1880s

(*Left*) Gnarled trees in the park, relics of ancient woodland at Calke

The last substantial addition to the park, called the 'New Park', was made by Sir John Harpur Crewe in 1875. Since then little progressive work has been done. Indeed, the parkland in Melbourne parish was severed from the main body of the park by the construction of the Staunton Harold reservoir in 1957–64, drowning some of the low-lying land near Calke Mill.

Since the park has opened its gates to more than just privileged visitors or the tenantry, it has been found to be one of the best parks in Britain for insects, mainly beetles. They occur in the old trees, in the bracken glades between, and around the ponds nearby. Analogy with primeval forests in Europe suggests that the species are direct descendants of our original 'wildwood' fauna. They depend for their survival on unbroken continuity of wooded cover, the woodland always containing old trees. This they have at Calke: the gnarled park trees are descended from the medieval woods from which the park was created, and these themselves were relics of the original forest cover. Sir Vauncey would have been delighted to learn that the old trees and their insects thus provide a direct link with the Derbyshire forests of 5000BC.

PONDS

The chain of curiously named ponds at Calke is mainly the result of work in the eighteenth and early nineteenth centuries. China House Pond, however, is probably medieval, and was known in the seventeenth century as Castle Pool, after Cheriston Castle (see above). It owes its present name to a long-vanished summer-house called the 'Chinese House', built on the island in the pond in 1747. Betty's Pond was originally created in 1741 and later enlarged. 'Betty', who gave her name to the pond, is yet to be identified. Thatch House Pond, referred to as the 'new pool' in 1752, is a reminder of Lady Catherine's Bower. The Bower,

now represented only by a raised circular foundation on the north side of the pond, was named after Catherine Crewe, who married Sir John Harpur in 1702, and presumably built for her. Mere Pond was created in the opening years of the nineteenth century, and completed the chain. On its northern bank, behind the foundation of a former boathouse, is a small brick-lined alcove, referred to in the nineteenth century, no doubt spuriously, as an 'ancient monk's cave'. Little Dogkennel Pond was named after the kennels which originally stood alongside it. Formerly it drained out into Big Dogkennel Pond, built in 1779–81 and now flooded by the Staunton Harold reservoir.

THE STABLES AND FARM BUILDINGS

The quadrangular stables at Calke were built in 1712–14 for Sir John Harpur by William Gilks, a master-builder from Burton-on-Trent who probably designed them. The original stalls and mangers in the southern range are mostly intact, separated by stout columns supporting arcades. The tack room on the east side of the courtyard has an evocative display of harness and saddles, its original oil lamps, and panelled cupboards, decorated with

The ponds in Calke Park

The Ticknall lime avenue in Calke Park, planted to celebrate the birth of the last Baronet, Sir Vauncey Harpur Crewe, in 1846

engravings and oleographs of race-horses. Not only were there stables, but also coach houses, granaries, store rooms and accommodation for servants such as grooms and coachmen. The iron weathervane on top of the stables was supplied in 1750 by Robert Bakewell.

The brew and bakehouses were moved from a building attached to the house to occupy part of the east range of the stables, probably in 1743. The two processes share common ingredients, so the brewhouse and the bakehouse were often staffed by the same man. Calke beer is reputed to have been good, although in 1815 Sir Henry Crewe expressed great dissatisfaction with both his brewer and his beer: 'you never see a drop sparkle in the glass and it tastes thick and sweet – what I like is a light fine ale; small beer should be brisk and fresh but not tart. As to the Baker, I caution you against any consultation with him. He is the man who has spoiled all my beer for the last 3 years . . . he is neither a good Baker nor a good Brewer . . . and I certainly do not mean to continue him.'

The brewhouse, connected to the ale and beer cellars of the house by a brick tunnel, contains considerable remains of the original equipment and is an interesting and rare survival.

The smithy, with a dovecote above, and the lean-to buildings flanking them, are contemporary with the main stable building. The smithy bellows still work, and the ceiling beams are charred where horseshoes have been hung on them to cool.

The rapid development of the stable buildings in the later eighteenth and early nineteenth centuries paralleled the growth of the park. The first substantial addition was the riding school, built to the designs of Joseph Pickford of Derby in 1767–9. It is a plain but impressive building, with huge roof trusses spanning 40 feet. The building reflects the great interest in horses shown by Sir Harry, but in 1777 the Harpur racehorse establishment was transferred to Swarkestone, which adjoined the Derby racecourse on Sinfin Moor. In the nineteenth century, the riding school was used to entertain estate tenants on special occasions.

Later additions include the fine, late eighteenth-century threshing barn, the chop house, open sheds, wagon hovel and joiner's shop. Like the black-smith's shop, the joiner's shop was almost untouched since it had last been used, many years before the Trust took it over in 1985: the tools were still in place, and window sashes lay on the benches awaiting repair.

THE PARISH CHURCH OF ST GILES

Calke Church, although it appears to be entirely nineteenth century, is a recasing of the Elizabethan building reputedly erected by Richard Wendsley, owner of Calke from c.1575 to 1585. Wendsley's church in turn seems to have replaced an earlier building which stood on part of the site of the present house. The sixteenth-century church was a relatively humble building without a tower, lit by plain, square-headed windows. The nave was separated from the chancel by a carved oak screen, and the bell hung at the west end in a wooden bellcote which by 1789 was in practice more like a pigeon house, 'whence cooing instead of bells must invite to prayer'.

This simple building nevertheless was a 'peculiar', enjoying the privilege of exemption from diocesan control, a status inherited from the days of the priory. This was a great advantage to Robert Bainbridge, who was an extreme Protestant. In the early seventeenth century, a popular non-

St Giles Church in Calke Park, remodelled by Sir George Crewe in 1827–9

Henry Cheere's monument to Sir John Harpur, 4th Baronet, and his wife, Catherine Crewe, erected in 1746

chancel screen, font cover, altar rail and an enclosed pew, survive, though sawn up and incomplete, in a room over the stables. No architect is known for the new church, and in the circumstances perhaps it did not require one.

The interior contains a fine monument by Henry Cheere to Sir John Harpur and his wife Catherine Crewe, erected in 1746. There are also monuments to Sir John Harpur Crewe and his son, Sir Vauncey, while Sir George Crewe is commemorated by the stained-glass window at the east end. In the gallery there is an interesting early nineteenth-century barrel-organ, complete with a set of barrels.

Some members of the family are buried in the vault under the church floor; others are buried in the churchyard along with many loyal family servants. The terrace running along the north and east sides of the churchyard was created by Sir George Crewe in 1832, and was one of his favourite places. The lime avenue connecting the churchyard to the pleasure ground was probably planted around the same time.

THE GARDENS AND PLEASURE GROUND

The walled gardens at Calke, covering about 7 acres, played an important part in the domestic economy of Calke. The small flower garden, known in the last century as 'Lady Crewe's Garden', was indeed maintained principally for visual effect, but the other parts of the garden were expected to earn their keep and concern was expressed when they did not. The Calke head gardener was no ordinary labourer: he needed to be intelligent, methodical and infinitely resourceful. He was expected to keep the grounds in order and to provide constant supplies of fruit, vegetables and flowers to the house all the year round. It was thought perfectly reasonable that he should provide a bouquet of flowers at short notice in January for a wedding. The gardener was also in charge of keeping the bees. In the 1830s, John Vernon, the head gardener, was assisted by a staff of about seven men and three women, although during harvest-time the garden staff were expected to help on the home farm.

Several members of the family, notably the Rev.

conformist preacher called Herring was employed at Calke, and several people from surrounding parishes built seats in the church in order to attend his services.

The church was remodelled in 1827–9 by Sir George Crewe, who found the old building 'dark, damp, out of repair, and possessing neither elegance or comfort'. The sum of £1,764 was spent in 'rendering it such a building as should at least show that outwardly the Lords House was not despised or forgotten'. A new tower of brick cased in stone was added, and the body of the church was refaced by a team of Melbourne masons under their master, William Chambers. The cast-iron windows were provided by Weatherhead, Glover & Co. of Derby, and John Harrison, also of Derby, installed a hot-air heating system. The roof trusses of the old church were reused, and fragments of Elizabethan woodwork appear in the dado at the east end. Many of the former fittings removed in 1827, including the

Henry Harpur Crewe, rector of Drayton Beauchamp in Buckinghamshire, and Georgiana, Lady Crewe have been plant collectors and cultivators. By the 1820s there were 58 varieties of geranium at Calke, including one named 'Calkensis', and another 'Crewensis'. These were ephemeral hybrids, but a small yellow wallflower named *Cheiranthus* 'Harpur Crewe' was rescued from extinction by the Rev. Harpur Crewe in Buckinghamshire in the late nineteenth century and is still widely grown. He was also responsible for raising *Doronicum* 'Harpur Crewe', (correctly *D. plantagineum* 'Excelsum'), and *Crocus biflorus*, subsp. *crewei*. A variety of narcissus known as the 'Findern Flower' is said to have been brought back from the Holy Land by a crusading ancestor of Jane Findern, who married Richard Harpur in the 1540s. The Findern Flowers are still to be found in the Derbyshire village of Findern, near the site of the family's manor house, and it is hoped that they will be successfully reintroduced to Calke.

The present walled gardens were built in 1773 in the nook of the large tract of land added to the park in 1769. Screened from the house by a plantation to avoid interference with the picturesque view from the east front, they are now approached along a path to the gardeners' bothy flanked in summer by sweet peas and dahlias. The bothy still contains traditional fittings, such as a seed cabinet with many small drawers. The layout of the walled gardens, slightly irregular due to constraints imposed by earlier boundaries, comprises a small flower garden, a physic garden and a large kitchen garden with a narrow 'slip' garden on its southern and western sides. Originally there was also an orchard, retained from the early eighteenth-century layout, which disappeared in the nineteenth century: only a few fruit trees and fragments of the stone-built orchard wall survive. However, a short avenue of early eighteenth-century limes that once screened the orchard from the house still remains, and was incorporated into the present plantations when the new gardens were built.

The flower garden was enlarged to the south in the first half of the nineteenth century, and its basic layout is of that period. It is planted in a mid-nineteenth-century manner with borders predominantly of herbaceous plants lining the walls in the 'mingled' style favoured by the nineteenth-century horticulturalist J. C. Loudon. The beds in the central lawn are arranged geometrically and planted to resemble Victorian bedding, while the basket bed south of the main lawn is a typically Victorian feature. On the south-facing wall are the flower house and aviary, and in the north-west corner is an alcove with tiered shelving, formerly used to display auriculas and other potted plants, possibly the last surviving auricula theatre.

The Auricula Theatre in the flower garden. In spring it would display auriculas, and in summer geraniums, hydrangeas and other pot plants

The physic garden, originally intended for the cultivation of medicinal herbs, was still so called in the 1930s, though it was then much more commonly referred to as the Lower Kitchen Garden. On its north side are the stove house, built in 1785, and the vinery, probably from 1810. The vinery was originally twice its present size, but the heating of the eastern half was discontinued in 1931 and the western half was demolished after the Second World War. The physic garden also contains several pits and frames originally used for growing cucumbers, melons, pineapples and violets. It is still used as a kitchen garden, growing historical varieties of fruit and vegetables, many of them available when the garden was first created.

The 4-acre kitchen garden, or Upper Kitchen Garden, is by far the largest section. Now little more than an empty paddock, partly as a result of post-war economy measures, it was once a curious mixture of the ornamental and the practical, divided into regular plots by a grid of paths. The last vestiges of this layout were swept away in the 1970s. Three ornamental circular ponds and a nineteenth-century summer-house still survive, along with some old fruit trees trained up the walls.

At the centre of the gardens is the building that houses the conservatory, gardeners' rooms and fruit stores, built in 1777 and originally flanked by matching greenhouses. The iron and glass dome of the conservatory, dismantled many years ago and awaiting restoration, was added by John Harrison of Derby in 1837 for Sir George Crewe. The western greenhouse has been demolished, but the eastern one was rebuilt with a reduced span by Colonel and Mrs Mosley in 1930.

The extensive pleasure ground surrounding the house is separated from the park by a sunken wall, allowing uninterrupted views into the park while preventing the entry of deer and cattle. Like parts of the park, it consists of large, informal expanses of grass dotted with specimen trees, but it differs from the park in containing a wide variety of exotic trees, delicate shrubs and carpets of spring-flowering bulbs, which need protection against grazing animals. Most of the shrubs were sheltered in the plantations around the perimeter of the pleasure ground, interspersed by winding, gravelled paths.

The pleasure ground occupies the site of the early eighteenth-century formal gardens, laid out under the guidance of the royal gardeners London and Wise at the time of the rebuilding of the house. In 1710–15, a new garden was created on the east front, following the payment of £5 7s. 6d. to 'Mr Coke ye Gardainer for his Draughts' in January 1710. This was perhaps the William Cook who laid out the famous garden at Melbourne in 1704 under instructions from London and Wise. The new garden, later

The Physic or Lower Kitchen Garden with frames for growing exotic fruits and vegetables

The interior of gardener's room in the Upper Kitchen Garden built in the late eighteenth century. Each drawer in the cabinet was assigned to a different kind of vegetable seed

known as the 'best garden', was enclosed by brick walls and included flights of stone stairs, alcoves and ornamental ironwork by Robert Bakewell.

Unfortunately, the only illustrative evidence of the formal grounds at Calke is the plan of the parish made in 1761. The plan marks the walls of the 'best garden', which is represented today by the level platform on the east front. To the south, on the bank, there was a square garden with paths radiating from its centre, and further east there was an orchard and a cherry orchard. Formal gardens were notoriously expensive to maintain and, like the avenues in the park, they disappeared in the 1770s when they had become conveniently old-fashioned. The formation of the pleasure ground by Sir Harry Harpur is apparently unrecorded, but parts of the sunken wall contain carved stones, no doubt reused from structures in the formal gardens.

In 1816–17 Sir Henry Crewe extended the pleasure ground to the east, erecting iron gates and railings at its two main entrances. At the same time a new carriage road was built through the pleasure ground and out into the eastern part of the park, passing over a three-arched Gothic bridge to a new lodge opposite Melbourne Coppice. The bridge was sadly demolished in the 1960s to make way for the Staunton Harold reservoir. Another feature of the work carried out in 1816–17 was a tunnel built

for the gardeners to pass from the walled garden into the park. The tunnel passed under the pleasure ground plantation, and was built so that Sir Henry, with his obsession for seclusion, could stroll at leisure in the plantation without disturbance from the gardeners and other servants.

The layout of the pleasure ground has changed little since Sir Henry's time, but a vast amount of damage has been wrought to the planting by the red and fallow deer which were latterly permitted to graze here. The deer are now restricted to an enclosure in the north-east corner of the park and new planting is being undertaken, using varieties popular during the mid-nineteenth century.

The only important building in the pleasure ground is the grotto, built for Sir Henry in 1809 by an architect from Derby, Samuel Browne. It is a good example of its kind, incorporating panels of artificial Coade stone, and is awaiting restoration. There are slight remains of another possible grotto of uncertain date adjoining an old quarry face in the plantation leading to the walled gardens.

The conservatory built in 1777 by John Harrison of Derby

CHAPTER EIGHT
THE ESTATE

The Harpur estate in South Derbyshire was founded by Richard Harpur in the sixteenth century. As a successful lawyer, he could usefully observe the traffic in land and manorial rights to decide how best to invest his money. His immediate ancestors were the lords of Rushall in Staffordshire, and he acquired the nucleus of the estate by his marriage in the mid-1540s to Jane Findern. The Finderns had long been established in the village of the same name, and Jane became heiress to their estate on the death of her brother in 1558. Richard Harpur built a new house at Swarkestone, consolidating the estate whenever an opportunity presented itself. He also bought land at Alstonefield in Staffordshire that became the nucleus of an important secondary estate.

Calke was bought for his grandson, Henry Harpur, in 1622 as part of a family settlement. Several deaths in the Harpur family in the seventeenth century meant that Sir John was able to inherit combined estates that eventually amounted to some 34,000 acres, 20,000 in Staffordshire, 13,000 in Derbyshire and 877 at Hemington in Leicestershire.

In many places the Finderns and the Harpurs had taken over smaller estates with their own manor houses; these often became redundant and several were eventually destroyed. Even the family's own ancestral homes were not spared. The manor house at Findern was demolished, and Richard Harpur's grand Elizabethan house at Swarkestone suffered the same fate in the mid-eighteenth century. The banqueting house at Swarkestone, an attractive building of the 1630s was, however, allowed to remain and has recently been restored by the Landmark Trust. Some of the fittings from Swarkestone were taken to Calke in the 1740s and are said to include the magnificent Elizabethan chimney-piece now in one of Mr Henry Harpur-Crewe's private rooms.

The National Trust's Calke Abbey estate was cut from the kernel of the Harpur-Crewe South Derbyshire estate in 1985 to provide an endowment for the house and park, and to preserve the landscape to the south as far as the Pistern Hills. It comprises over 2,000 acres of land, mainly in the parishes of Calke, Ticknall and Ashby-de-la-Zouch.

The southern end of this estate was only acquired by the Harpur-Crewe family comparatively recently, and some land on the northern side, formerly part of a Crown woodland known as Derby Hills, was purchased by Sir Vauncey Harpur Crewe from the Melbourne Hall estate in 1919. The land at the southern end is known as Southwood, another former medieval woodland, which is divided into two parts: the western part, lying in

Chessboard pattern of places on the Harpur Crewe estate, probably by G. R. Vawser, who taught art to the Harpur Crewe children in the early 1860s. The subjects include Calke Abbey, the grotto and the banqueting house at Swarkestone

Elizabethan chimneypiece with the Harpur arms, in Henry Harpur-Crewe's private apartment at Calke. This chimneypiece is believed to have come from the family house at Swarkestone

Derbyshire and acquired by Sir George Crewe through an exchange in 1821, consists of farmland overshadowed by the long, sinuous Pistern Hills Plantation, created c.1825 partly as a feature on the horizon when viewed from Calke Park; the eastern part, in Leicestershire, is still wooded and was purchased by Sir Vauncey in 1900. It contains concentrations of small, primitive coal mines known as bell-pits.

The Harpur Crewe association with the central part of the estate is of much longer standing. The Harpur family were principal landowners in Ticknall from 1616, and were sole owners of Calke parish from 1622. Ticknall village lies just outside the National Trust boundary and part of it remains in family ownership.

TICKNALL VILLAGE

A visitor to Ticknall in 1789 described it as a long straggling village. It has two main streets, with the parish church near their junction. The manorial history of Ticknall is confusing and complicated; for the purposes of this short account it is enough to suggest that the two main lines of settlement may represent the adjoining settlements of separate estates or manors. Certainly, early seventeenth-century Ticknall still had two manor houses called the 'Nether Hall' and the 'Over Hall', neither of which survives today.

Ticknall is first recorded in the opening years of the eleventh century in the form 'Ticenheale', the goat kids' nook in the woods. This sounds fanciful, but the area was well wooded until Elizabeth I's time, when goat herds could still be found there. Sixteenth- and seventeenth-century Ticknall, like many other South Derbyshire parishes, lay amid its three great arable open fields: Knowl Hill Field, Calke or Little Field, and Park Field, named after Foremark Park. These fields, and the extensive common lands around Ticknall, were eaten away by piecemeal enclosure in the sixteenth and seventeenth centuries, and the enclosure of the parish was completed by private agreement in 1764–5.

By this time, over three-quarters of the land in Ticknall already belonged to the Harpurs of Calke. Sir John Harpur of Swarkestone had bought a large estate in Ticknall in 1616 for £900, and the ascendancy of the Harpurs was enhanced by the disappearance of the Francis and Abel families, the village's most important medieval landowners. By the nineteenth century, virtually everyone in Ticknall worked on the Harpur Crewe estate, but the Harpurs were never the sole owners. One of the houses in High Street, once a draper's shop, is surmounted by the surname 'Sheffield' carved in large stone letters, like a mute demonstration against the Harpur Crewe monopoly.

The estate, particularly in the nineteenth and early twentieth centuries, was largely a self-contained unit, and this was most clearly demonstrated when new buildings were constructed. Local architects were employed, such as Seth Smith of Repton, Henry Isaac Stevens of Derby or John

Shaw of Derby, who became the Harpur Crewe estate agent in 1872. Sometimes new buildings were built by the estate's own army of bricklayers, carpenters and joiners, dominated by the Marriott family, but if work was in progress on many buildings simultaneously, contracts were made with local building firms such as the Bridgarts of Derby, John Wood of Derby and Bullock and Barton of Melbourne.

The estate was able to supply most of its own materials. Until the 1860s, the two Ticknall brickyards run by the Hill and Smart families produced countless numbers of bricks, paving bricks, tiles and drainage pipes, which were distributed to all parts of the South Derbyshire estate. Local farmers provided straw for thatching, and the estate plantations were systematically managed to produce a good supply of timber. Sometimes, young saplings were brought in from local nurserymen and planted out direct. An alternative was to buy in seedlings, which were then raised in the estate's own nursery plantations before being transplanted. When felled, timber was taken on drags to the woodyard at Ticknall, where it was seasoned and sawn. The wettest parts of the plantations were planted as osier beds, which were let to local basketmakers.

Plantations were normally established on land that was difficult to work, either because the soil was unsuitable or because the surface was steep. Plantations also provided game cover and might be planted with this in mind. Shaw's Plantation, for example, was originally created in 1878 when it was planted with 11,100 shrubs. Dark Plantation in Calke Park was known as the 'Dark Cover', and was formerly planted with coniferous trees. Other large plantations were created at Hill Close (now called Clay Pit Plantation) in 1878 and at Church Close, Gilbert's Meadow and Town Leys (collectively called Jubilee Plantation) in 1887–9.

The limitations imposed on the estate's self-sufficiency were partly determined by its geological resources and restricted industrialisation. The Ticknall brick kilns were lined with fire-bricks produced nearby at Woodville, as there was no fire clay at Ticknall, and cast-iron goods such as kitchen ranges and brickmaking machinery were purchased from local foundries such as Thornewill and Warham's

at Burton-on-Trent or R. Russell and Sons at Derby. The Ticknall blacksmith, who had a forge near the lime yards, would produce simpler wrought-iron goods such as cramps, strap-hinges and latches, using bought-in bar iron. Stone for lintels and hearths was obtained from the millstone-grit outcrop in the parishes of Melbourne and Stanton by Bridge.

The last three baronets showed a paternalistic attitude to their tenantry. Sir George made a habit of visiting his tenants personally, paying particular attention to those that threatened to err from the path of a good Christian life. Alternatively, his tenants would arrange to visit Sir George at Calke. One such visit is recorded in his diary for 26 November 1825: 'Beighton's wife, Ticknall, gave her a severe reprimand for her dirty, slovenly habits, and earnestly entreated [her] to think of the awful consequences of bringing up her family in idleness . . . gave her 5 shillings, but desired her never to come again unless she first made herself and children more decent and fit to be seen.' Judicious bene-

Cast-iron stand pipe installed in Ticknall village by Sir Vauncey Harpur Crewe in 1914

volence of a similar kind was practised by the 10th Earl Ferrers of nearby Staunton Harold, who presented every newly married servant with furniture for a comfortable sitting room, considering 'that nothing contributed so materially to wedded happiness'.

Ticknall is full of reminders of Harpur Crewe patronage and influence. The fir trees in pairs on either side of the road were planted in 1876 to commemorate the marriage of Sir Vauncey Harpur Crewe to Isabel Adderley, and the attractive cast-iron stand-pipes or 'taps' were installed by Sir Vauncey in 1914. He also set up a Reading Room with its own library, provided a cricket ground, and gave the site of the village hall, an ex-First World War army hut. Within memory, the joinery of the irregular rows of cottages was uniformly painted white and stone colour, while the garden gates were painted green. Many of the houses still have stylistic idiosyncrasies, including round-cornered chimney-stacks, which show that the Calke estate builders have been at work on them.

The administration of the South Derbyshire estate was controlled from the woodyard at Ticknall, which accommodated the estate office, saw-pit and joiners' shops (though John Shaw's office was in Derby). Thomas Grime, agent for the estate between 1841 and 1872, lived in a house near the church from which he could keep close watch on the village. The estate workforce, based here, would travel daily to the outlying parts of the estate. However, owing to their remoteness from Calke, and in some cases to the presence of other important landowners in the area, the Harpur Crewe presence in these places was less strongly felt than in Ticknall. Mr Leslie Cox of Twyford, agent for the Harpur-Crewe estate from 1960–9, remembers that as a small boy he knew that the village belonged to a greatly respected lady called Mrs Mosley of Calke, which lay somewhere beyond the hills in the distance.

The present parish church at Ticknall was built largely at the expense of Sir George Crewe in 1841–2, to designs by Henry Isaac Stevens. The earlier fourteenth-century church, dedicated to St Thomas à Becket, was considered too small, and it should be borne in mind that Ticknall's population in the

1830s was at its largest ever, 1,278 in 1831. In January 1834, it was suddenly discovered that the old church was too dangerous for the public to enter, and Sir George took this as a 'warning that we should build a better temple to the glory of God'. In the same year, the churchyard was extended and a site was reserved for the proposed new church.

The old church is still known through drawings and descriptions. It had a tower and spire, and the figures of Time and Death were painted at the ends of the aisles. Following the demolition of the main body of the church, the tower and spire were blown up before an assembled crowd at quarter to six on 5 September 1841. An emotional witness wrote that the scene 'was truly affecting to behold and produced many awful and solemn reflections with tears'. Two fragments of the old church still remain: the south-west corner of the tower and the east window of the north aisle. The new church was dedicated to St George, believed by some to be a compliment to Sir George Crewe, who was long remembered as a kind, fair and generous landlord. The row of seven almshouses on Church Lane, erected in 1772, is another monument to Harpur philanthropy, built to provide homes for seven decayed housekeepers from Ticknall and Calke.

If a long association with the Harpur Crewes is one of Ticknall's distinguishing features, the other is its renown for the production of pottery and lime. The pottery works were concentrated at the southern end of the village, on the edge of the former common lands situated on the Upper Coal Measures, which provided a source of clay. Some of the irregular clusters of houses here seem to owe their existence to the pottery industry, which appears to be exceptional for being rural-based and a cottage industry. The potters seem to have hit on a way of successfully firing large vessels, and North Derbyshire lead for use in glazes was conveniently near.

There is no certain evidence for a medieval pottery here, but by the late sixteenth century 'Ticknall ware' was well known. Writing in 1650, the Derbyshire historian Philip Kynder exclaimed that 'Here are your best Fictilias [pottery goods] made you, earthen vessels, potts and pancions at Tycknall, and carried all East England through'. Much of the

A plate in Ticknall ware, from Sir John Harpur Crewe's collection at Calke Abbey

pottery produced at Ticknall was coarse and primitive, but surviving pieces also include figurines and decorated slipware. Ticknall was still famous for the production of earthenware in the early eighteenth century, but by 1789 it was noted that 'lately business has much declined'. It was said that the enclosure of Ticknall in 1764–5 had led to a scarcity of good potting clay, but it is likely that the Staffordshire pottery industry was already beginning to eclipse the enterprise.

The last of the Ticknall potteries, at Pottery House (SK348228), did not close until 1891, but nineteenth-century Ticknall products were mainly unrefined objects such as flower and chimney pots. Pottery House seems to have been the pottery known as 'Mire Oak' in the seventeenth century. Other pottery sites have been identified at SK344228 (formerly known as Hazard Hill and later used as a smallpox hospital) and SK346226 (formerly known as Prince Wood). In the mid-eighteenth century there was a pottery near the centre of the village.

While the enclosure movement of the second half of the eighteenth century may have caused the decline of Ticknall's pottery industry, it also brought about the most prosperous period of the village's lime-burning industry. Enclosure led to a great demand for lime as a land improver, and Ticknall contains one of the few limestone outcrops that occur several miles south of the main North Derbyshire beds. Lime burning is documented at Ticknall as far back as 1462, and in the seventeenth and eighteenth centuries it was dominated by a series of Gilbert Hutchinsons. As time passed, the Ticknall lime burners were bought out by the Harpur Crewe estate, and the Hutchinson family were tenants of Sir George Crewe when they finally went bankrupt in the mid-1830s. The limeworks were next let to John Foster, who was also unable to make a success of them. Foster gave the works up in 1843, when he was paid an award of £2,735 7s. 2d. by Sir George.

In 1771, an attempt to turnpike the road from Hartshorne to Swarkestone Bridge was resisted by some people because it was feared that toll-gates would inhibit the Ticknall lime trade. But 30 years later a tramway was built by Benjamin Outram to link up with a new canal near Ashby. The tramway bridge at Ticknall, commonly called 'the Arch', is Ticknall's best-known landmark. These improvements in transport reflect the growing importance of the Ticknall lime trade, which reached its peak in the 1830s despite the difficulties faced by its proprietors.

In the 1840s, however, the extraction of limestone was becoming more difficult: a pumping engine was required to keep the works drained and thick overlying strata had to be penetrated before the limestone could be reached. The last tenant of the works was William Garrard, also the village's veterinary surgeon, and his widow gave up the works in the 1880s. Thereafter, only one or two kilns were kept in operation to provide lime for estate purposes. Parts of the lime yards were deliberately planted in the late nineteenth century as the backdrop to a new addition to Calke Park, and lime production finally ceased in 1940. Since then, nature has rapidly taken hold of the abandoned workings. Amid the tangled undergrowth, the visitor encounters unexpected vistas of banks of kilns, stretches of tramway, exposed rock faces and old quarries flooded with dark, still water. The quarrying was very deep: twelve to fifteen yards was quite common.

The Ticknall limeworks are probably more remarkable today than they were 150 years ago. They are a fascinating and rare survival, intimately associated with early transport technology. In many places, old limeworks have long since disappeared to make way for more modern techniques, but the exhaustion and long abandonment of the Ticknall works has saved them from this fate. The survival of the brickworks across the road, opposite the limeworks, is also uncommon. Most parishes with suitable clay deposits had brickyards, but Ticknall continued to produce bricks until 1940, and the Victorian machinery and kiln were used until the end.

The decline of Ticknall in the nineteenth century has paradoxically contributed much to the character of the village; as lime burning dwindled, there was nothing to replace it and keep people in the village, so very little building work took place after the 1840s. Old houses were repaired and re-roofed, but the streetscape remains predominantly eighteenth century. Between 1851 and 1901 Ticknall lost an average of ten people every year. For a village of less than 1,300 people, the loss of 500 inhabitants in 50 years was dramatic and many houses, particu-

larly on the fringes of the village, were demolished. By 1961 the population had sunk to only 535.

CALKE VILLAGE

Calke village is nothing more than an attractive hamlet on the brow of a hill overlooking the Staunton Harold reservoir. Excluding Calke Abbey, the Home Farm and Heathend Lodge, it contains a farmhouse and six other houses, most of which are huddled in the shelter offered by the screen belt of the park. The houses have changed relatively little in the last hundred years, and the construction of the reservoir in 1957–64 has caused the village street to become a quiet cul-de-sac.

It comes therefore as something of a surprise to learn that the mid-sixteenth-century householders of Calke comprised John Prest Esquire at the manor house, two millers, a widow, six husbandmen, seven labourers and a minstrel. These people, with their households, represent a population of about 80. But where did they live, and what happened to their homes?

The best answer to the first question is provided by the 1761 plan of Calke. This plan, with its accompanying reference book, suggests that Calke

Calke Mill, which disappeared in the 1960s to make way for Staunton Harold Reservoir

The Home Farm at Calke, from a photograph taken in the 1880s

had changed remarkably little over the preceding two centuries. Including Calke Abbey and the Dairy House on the western edge of the park, Calke still contained seventeen houses and its population was composed largely of husbandmen and labourers. The tenants of some of the smaller holdings worked at the Home Farm at Calke, as their predecessors in the sixteenth century had no doubt done.

The plan also affords some evidence about the origins of the village, and lends support to the argument that the foundation of the priory preceded the development of the village; in the seventeenth and eighteenth centuries, all of the land let to tenants at Calke was situated along the eastern and southern sides of the parish, and the houses were scattered across the tenanted land. Calke was not then a nucleated compact village, and the present village of Calke represents the largest of three former focuses of settlement in the parish. The Home Farm land consisted of larger fields near the manor house, which probably followed the crop rotation of a normal open-field system. All this suggests that the land on the fringes of the parish was leased by the Prior of Repton or the Cellarer of Calke to laymen who

built houses there when monastic vocations declined in the later Middle Ages.

It was the expansion of Calke Park during the late eighteenth century that led to the partial destruction of Calke village. From the 1760s onwards, farmland was taken into the park as the tenants died or left, and the demolition of the farmhouses followed naturally. One of the redundant farmhouses was converted in 1780 to become the new Dairy House (now Home Farm), which provided milk, butter, cheese, eggs and poultry for Calke Abbey until the early twentieth century. This house once stood on the village street, but in 1779 the northern part of the street was taken into the park. A new length of road was built to replace it, which is the present straight road from the thatched cottages at Calke village to the circular car park overlooking the reservoir.

By the early nineteenth century, the two smaller focuses of settlement in the parish had virtually disappeared; one of them was represented only by Calke parsonage on the western edge of the parish, which had been converted from a redundant farmhouse in 1766 and was pulled down in 1879. The other was represented by Calke Mill, the mill house and a cottage nearby, all of which were demolished and flooded in the 1960s when the reservoir was built.

89

GROUND FLOOR

The room names are taken from documentary sources of the 1830s and 1840s, except for the Laundry Stairs, which are later. Most of the names have not changed since.

Hatched walls have been added since the rebuilding of 1701–4

Dotted lines indicate walls removed since the rebuilding of 1701–4.

Minor alterations to fireplaces etc. are not indicated.

1 ENTRANCE HALL. Created 1842.
2 BEST STAIRS.
3 THE LOBBY. This is the surviving eastern half of the ground-floor entrance passage of 1701–4
4 THE CARICATURE ROOM.
5 GARDEN ENTRANCE. External door now replaced by a window.
6 BOTTOM STUDY. Remodelled in 1809 and again in the 1820s or '30s. Used by Sir Henry Crewe, Sir George Crewe, Mr Richard F. M. Crewe and Colonel Mosley.
7 THE BLUE ROOM.
8 'BEDLAM'.
9 GUN ROOM.

10 BUTLER'S BEDROOM.
11 SERVANTS' HALL.
12 SHOE HOUSE.
13 ALE and BEER CELLARS.
14 WINE CELLAR.
15 OLD BREWHOUSE. Probably discontinued as a brewhouse in 1743.
16 THE LAUNDRY STAIRS. Constructed in 1866.
17 KITCHEN. Created 1794. Discontinued in the 1920s.
18 LARDERS.
19 STEWARD'S ROOM and EVIDENCE ROOM. Probably created in the 1830s.

20 PORTER'S ROOM.
21 HOUSEKEEPER'S SITTING ROOM. Created 1794. Formerly kitchen.
22 STILL ROOM. Converted into a kitchen 1928.
23 STEWARD'S ROOM. Used as a study by Sir J. H. Crewe and Sir V. H. Crewe. Used as a dining-room since the 1920s.
24 BILLIARD ROOM. Created 1842. Formerly Evidence Room.
25 STONE STAIRS. Built 1842. Formerly the 'White Stairs'.

FIRST FLOOR

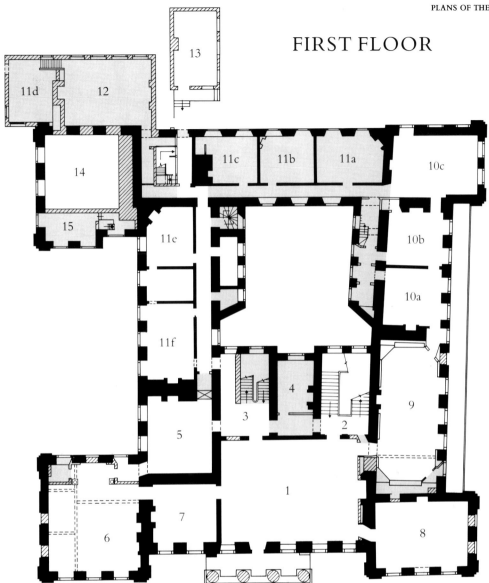

1 SALOON. Formerly known as the Great Hall.
2 BEST STAIRS.
3 STONE STAIRS.
4 OLD BUTLER'S PANTRY. Discontinued 1794.
5 BUTLER'S PANTRY. Created 1794. Formerly upper part of the kitchen.
6 DINING ROOM. Created 1794. Formerly divided to form the 'Gilt Leather' apartment.
7 BREAKFAST ROOM. Refitted 1810. Formerly known as the Little Dining Parlour.

8 DRAWING ROOM. Refitted 1794. Formerly the Dining Room.
9 LIBRARY. Created 1805. Formerly the Drawing Room.
10 Apartment occupied by Sir George and Lady Crewe. Rooms refitted in early nineteenth century.
  (a) LADY CREWE'S SITTING ROOM. Formerly the Inner Drawing Room.
  (b) SIR GEORGE CREWE'S DRESSING ROOM.
  (c) SIR GEORGE and LADY CREWE'S BEDROOM. Later the Schoolroom.

11 Servants' Rooms:
  (a) LADY'S MAID'S ROOM.
  (b) COOK'S BEDROOM.
  (c) HOUSEMAID'S SITTING ROOM. This was the laundry until 1812.
  (d) LAUNDRY BEDROOM.
  (e) HOUSEKEEPER'S BEDROOM, now a museum room.
  (f) HOUSEMAID'S BEDROOM, now displaying the Calke State Bed.
12 LAUNDRY. Constructed on top of an earlier building in 1812.
13 WASH HOUSE. Constructed in 1812.
14 Upper part of kitchen.
15 STORE ROOM over Cook's Closet.

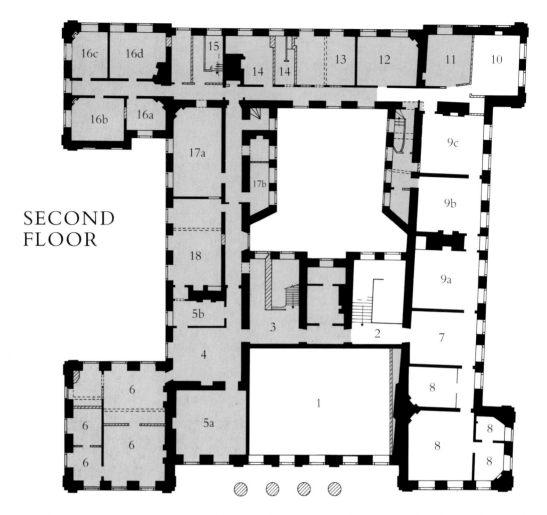

SECOND
FLOOR

1 Upper part of Saloon.

2 BEST STAIRS.

3 STONE STAIRS.

4 LOBBY. Refitted in the late eighteenth century.

5 Rooms occupied by Sir John Harpur, 4th Bart., (d.1741)
(a) THE PINK BEDROOM. Refitted in late eighteenth century.
(b) THE PINK DRESSING ROOM. Fitted with reused seventeenth-century panelling.

6 LADY FRANCES HARPUR'S ROOMS. Named after Lady Frances Harpur (d.1825). These rooms were previously occupied by Lady Catherine Harpur (d.1745), wife of the 4th Baronet. They were remodelled in the late eighteenth century.

7 BIRD LOBBY. Refitted in the late eighteenth century.

8 THE OAK ROOMS. This was the apartment occupied by Sir Henry and Nanette, Lady Crewe, after their marriage in 1792. The rooms were refitted in the late eighteenth century.

9 Apartment occupied by Sir Henry and Lady Caroline Harpur 1741–8.
(a) THE JAPANNED BEDROOM. Formerly Lady Harpur's Dressing Room.
(b) NURSERY BEDROOM. Formerly Sir Henry and Lady Harpur's Bedroom. Original joinery intact.
(c) NURSERY SITTING ROOM. Formerly Sir Henry Harpur's Dressing Room. Original joinery intact.

10 SCHOOL ROOM, later Mr Vauncey Harpur Crewe's Bedroom.

11 MISS CREWE'S ROOM.

12 THE MATTED ROOM.

13 BATH ROOM. Created by Sir George Crewe, 1837. Converted back to bedroom 1866.

14 GOVERNESS'S BEDROOM. Converted into a bathroom 1866.

15 LAUNDRY STAIRS. Built 1866. A bedroom on the 'Bachelor's Passage' was dispensed with to make way for the new staircase.

16 BEDROOMS along the 'BACHELOR'S PASSAGE'. 16b was occupied by Mr Richard Harpur Crewe. 16d was occupied by Miss Wheldon, a nineteenth-century governess.

17 (a) THE YELLOW BEDROOM.
(b) THE YELLOW DRESSING ROOM.

18 SIR GEORGE CREWE'S STUDY. Fitted with reused seventeenth-century panelling.

FAMILY TREE

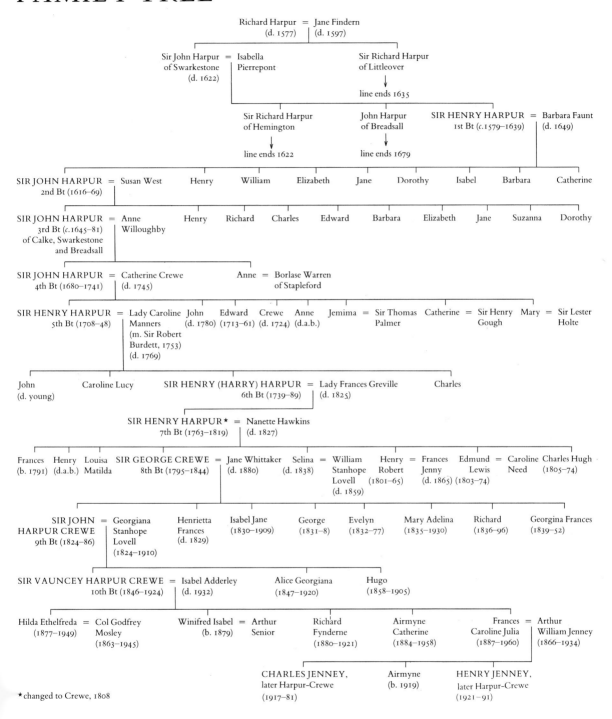

Richard Harpur = Jane Findern
(d. 1577) (d. 1597)

Sir John Harpur = Isabella
of Swarkestone   Pierrepont
(d. 1622)

Sir Richard Harpur
of Littleover
↓
line ends 1635

Sir Richard Harpur
of Hemington
↓
line ends 1622

John Harpur
of Breadsall
↓
line ends 1679

SIR HENRY HARPUR = Barbara Faunt
1st Bt (c.1579–1639)   (d. 1649)

SIR JOHN HARPUR = Susan West   Henry   William   Elizabeth   Jane   Dorothy   Isabel   Barbara   Catherine
2nd Bt (1616–69)

SIR JOHN HARPUR = Anne   Henry   Richard   Charles   Edward   Barbara   Elizabeth   Jane   Suzanna   Dorothy
3rd Bt (c.1645–81)   Willoughby
of Calke, Swarkestone
and Breadsall

SIR JOHN HARPUR = Catherine Crewe   Anne = Borlase Warren
4th Bt (1680–1741)   (d. 1745)   of Stapleford

SIR HENRY HARPUR = Lady Caroline   John   Edward   Crewe   Anne   Jemima = Sir Thomas   Catherine = Sir Henry   Mary = Sir Lester
5th Bt (1708–48)   Manners   (d. 1780) (1713–61) (d. 1724) (d.a.b.)   Palmer   Gough   Holte
                    (m. Sir Robert
                    Burdett, 1753)
                    (d. 1769)

John   Caroline Lucy   SIR HENRY (HARRY) HARPUR = Lady Frances Greville   Charles
(d. young)   6th Bt (1739–89)   (d. 1825)

SIR HENRY HARPUR ★ = Nanette Hawkins
7th Bt (1763–1819)   (d. 1827)

Frances   Henry   Louisa   SIR GEORGE CREWE = Jane Whittaker   Selina = William   Henry = Frances   Edmund = Caroline   Charles Hugh
(b. 1791) (d.a.b.) Matilda   8th Bt (1795–1844)   (d. 1880)   (d. 1838) Stanhope Robert Jenny   Lewis   Need   (1805–74)
                                                                           Lovell   (1801–65) (d. 1865) (1803–74)
                                                                           (d. 1859)

SIR JOHN = Georgiana   Henrietta   Isabel Jane   George   Evelyn   Mary Adelina   Richard   Georgina Frances
HARPUR CREWE Stanhope   Frances   (1830–1909)   (1831–8) (1832–77) (1835–1930)   (1836–96) (1839–52)
9th Bt (1824–86) Lovell   (d. 1829)
                 (1824–1910)

SIR VAUNCEY HARPUR CREWE = Isabel Adderley   Alice Georgiana   Hugo
10th Bt (1846–1924)   (d. 1932)   (1847–1920)   (1858–1905)

Hilda Ethelfreda = Col Godfrey   Winifred Isabel = Arthur   Richard   Airmyne   Frances = Arthur
(1877–1949)   Mosley   (b. 1879)   Senior   Fynderne   Catherine Caroline Julia William Jenney
                   (1863–1945)   (1880–1921) (1884–1958) (1887–1960)   (1866–1934)

CHARLES JENNEY,   Airmyne   HENRY JENNEY,
later Harpur-Crewe (b. 1919) later Harpur-Crewe
(1917–81)   (1921–91)

★ changed to Crewe, 1808

BIBLIOGRAPHY

The Harpur Crewe family papers are deposited in the Derbyshire County Record Office. The manuscripts and sketch-books of the Egyptologist Sir John Gardner Wilkinson (1797–1875) are deposited in the Bodleian Library, Oxford.

BIGGS, J. J., *The History and Antiquities of Hemington* (1873).

BIGSBY, Robert, *Historical and Topographical Description of Repton* (London, 1854).

COLVIN, Howard, 'Calke Priory', *Derbyshire Archaeological Journal*, CII, 1982.

COLVIN, Howard, 'Calke Abbey, Derbyshire', *Country Life*, 20 October, 27 October, 3 November, 1983.

COLVIN, Howard, *Calke Abbey, Derbyshire: a hidden house revealed* (George Philip, 1985).

FAREY, John, *General View of the Agriculture and Minerals of Derbyshire* (Board of Agriculture, 1811).

FARINGTON, Joseph, *The Farington Diary*, ed. James Greig, Vol. 7 (Hutchinson, 1927).

FROST, Christopher, *A History of British Taxidermy* (C. Frost, 1987).

GALBRAITH, Georgina, ed., *The Journal of the Rev. William Bagshaw Stevens* (Clarendon Press, 1965).

Gentleman's Magazine, N. S. Vol. 21, 1844, pp.199–201, memoir of Sir George Crewe.

GLOVER, Stephen, *The History, Gazetteer and Directory of the County of Derby*, ed. Thomas Noble, Vol. I (Derby, 1829).

LAING, Alastair, *In Trust for the Nation* (1995), pp.68–9, 190–1, 226–7.

LYSONS, Daniel, and Lysons, Samuel, *Magna Britannia*, Vol. 5: *Derbyshire* (London, 1817).

Parliament, History of, The House of Commons 1558–1603, ed. P. W. Hasler (1981); *1715–1754*, ed. Sir Lewis Namier and Sir John Brooke (HMSO, 1964).

PHILLIPS, Sir Richard, *A Personal Tour through the United Kingdom* (London, 1825), pp.92–4

PROCKTER, N. J. 'The Rev. Henry Harpur Crewe' *The Garden*, Vol. III, Part 10, October 1986.

WOOLLEY, William, *History of Derbyshire*, ed. C. Glover & P. Riden (Derbyshire Record Society, 1981).

The results of a comprehensive archaeological survey of the Calke estate have been compiled in internal National Trust reports kept at the Estates Office, Cirencester.

INDEX